THEY LOST THEIR HEADS!

WHAT HAPPENED TO WASHINGTON'S TEETH,
EINSTEIN'S BRAIN, AND OTHER FAMOUS BODY PARTS

To Alison,
and our friendship gate

First published in the United States of America in April 2018
by Bloomsbury Children's Books
www.bloomsbury.com

Bloomsbury is a registered trademark of Bloomsbury Publishing Plc

For information about permission to reproduce selections from this book, write to
Permissions, Bloomsbury Children's Books, 1385 Broadway, New York, New York 10018
Bloomsbury books may be purchased for business or promotional use.
For information on bulk purchases please contact Macmillan Corporate and
Premium Sales Department at specialmarkets@macmillan.com

Library of Congress Cataloging-in-Publication Data
available upon request
ISBN 978-0-8027-3745-8

Printed in China by C&C Offset Printing Co., Ltd., Shenzhen, Guangdong
2 4 6 8 10 9 7 5 3 1

All papers used by Bloomsbury Publishing, Inc., are natural, recyclable products
made from wood grown in well-managed forests. The manufacturing processes
conform to the environmental regulations of the country of origin.

THEY LOST THEIR HEADS!

WHAT HAPPENED TO WASHINGTON'S TEETH, EINSTEIN'S BRAIN, AND OTHER FAMOUS BODY PARTS

CARLYN BECCIA

BLOOMSBURY

NEW YORK LONDON OXFORD NEW DELHI SYDNEY

CONTENTS

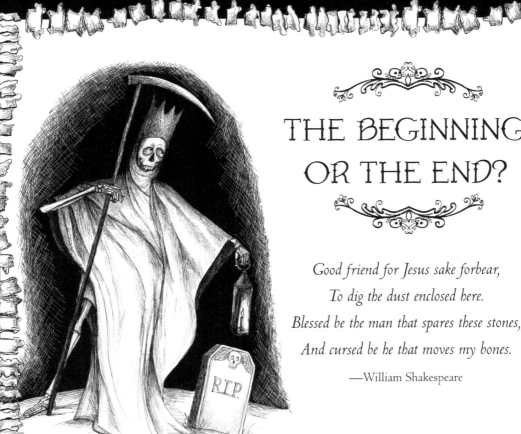

THE BEGINNING OR THE END?

Good friend for Jesus sake forbear,
To dig the dust enclosed here.
Blessed be the man that spares these stones,
And cursed be he that moves my bones.

—William Shakespeare

Let's begin with a quote from Shakespeare, because I know how much that will make you want to read this book. Everybody loves Shakespeare, right? The man was a freakin' genius. Wait . . . don't close the book yet. Yes, Shakespeare can be terribly dull with all that "'tis" and "thy" blathering, but there are also sword fights, witches brewing curses, and scary half-bird, half-man monsters. So there's that.

Still not convinced? Okay, okay. Shakespeare also wrote this creepy story about a guy named Hamlet, who was so psycho that he rescued a skull from a pile of bones and started talking to it like it was his new best friend. He even gave the skull a name—"Yorick." Now, that may sound like a bad example of genius writing, but from the moment the conversation began between Hamlet and his pet skull, something pretty amazing happened. Suddenly those twenty-two bones otherwise known as a human skull had new life, an identity . . . meaning. The skull had a story.

The stories in this book are intended to do just that—pull the dead from their graves and let them speak. The bodies of the people in this book did far more than just lie around with their flesh turning into maggot feed. Their parts were saved (or discarded) for all sorts of reasons. Sometimes out of love. Sometimes out of hate. Sometimes out of sheer curiosity, which is why most scientists dissect body parts today. In fact, if you were to die tomorrow, scientists could analyze your parts to determine your gender, age, and even if you ate too much junk food.

Of course, people are far more than just parts. The deceased live on in the people who loved them. Which is why I believe in conversations between the dead and the living. Every jarred heart, preserved bone, lopped-off ear, or lock of hair has a story to tell. So sit back, grab a snack, and let's hear what those rotting bits of flesh have to say.*

---

*You will find throughout this book that I take issue with talking about decomposing flesh on an empty stomach.

DEAD BODIES 101

I am guessing your science class didn't cover decomposition—how a body decays. Since it is the solid foundation for following the misadventures of famous body parts, we should get this part over with now.

TEMPERATURE

Everyone wants to live someplace warm, but when you die, it is best to head north. See, bodies are a lot like egg-salad sandwiches—the colder they're kept, the less likely they will stink over time.* The natural enzymes that break down food in your digestive tract continue to work after death. In warm weather, these enzymes work much faster. As tissue decays, a green mix of methane and hydrogen sulfide oozes out and creates a pretty bad stench. You probably wouldn't appreciate the smell, but maggots do. They start scooping up the green goo like icing off a cake.** Thus, the main reason why bodies fare better in the cold is because they smell less and, if they smell less, insects and animals can't find them. Which brings us to our next key factor in decomposition . . .

SCAVENGERS

Where there is a dead body, there are insects. Flesh flies are the first to the party. They will travel more than two miles to find a corpse and lay eggs on it. These eggs grow up to be adorable maggots and eventually . . . more

---

*My apologies for the food analogy. Unfortunately, I always seem to be writing about decomposition during lunch.
**Now it is time for dessert.

flies. In seven days, maggots will have feasted on 60 percent of a human body, unless other insects have spotted the corpse first and taken a few bites. After the flies, next come beetles, spiders, mites, and millipedes. If a body is not buried, larger animals (dogs, coyotes, wolves, and foxes) usually are close behind the insects. And while most birds lack a sense of smell, vultures can sniff out a dead body like hungry kids detecting freshly baked cookies.*

HUMIDITY

The dry climate is what really kept many Egyptian mummies so well preserved, although embalming techniques helped. The body contains millions of microscopic living organisms called bacteria. After death, they break down tissue in the body in a process called putrefaction. But bacteria need water to do this. Bodies exposed to water decompose four times faster than bodies in the earth.

FUN FACTS (UNLESS YOU ARE DEAD)

✓ Buried bodies are reduced to skeletons within forty years.

✓ Bodies exposed to the air will be reduced to skeletons in two to four weeks.

✓ Clothing speeds up decay.

✓ Skulls of younger adults decompose slower.

✓ The intestines are the first to rot. The brain, due to high water content, is next. Teeth and bones are the last.

Hmmm . . . Fresh bodies. Yum!

---

*While the rest of my food analogies have been entirely unnecessary, this one is not. Vultures really do prefer a fresh meal.

Inês de Castro

c.1325–January 7, 1355

TILL DEATH DO US PART

Despite what you may have read so far, I prefer not to begin a book with dismembered body parts. Instead we are going to start our adventure with a love story—a very haunting love story.*

This tale begins in Portugal with a noble lady named Inês de Castro. Inês was a real knockout. She had long blond hair and a graceful walk that earned her the epithet Colo de Garca ("Heron's Neck").** In 1340 Inês came to Portugal from Aragon as the lady-in-waiting and cousin to Constanza of Castile. Constanza had recently married the heir to the throne, Pedro I, but he just wasn't that into his new bride. Someone else caught his eye instead. He fell hopelessly in love with Constanza's cousin Inês.

Because of his infatuation, Pedro began to promote all of Inês's relatives to positions of power. This influence upset Pedro's father, King Alfonso IV, but he kept his mouth shut because he figured his son would tire of Inês soon.

Pedro did not tire of her. And when Constanza died in 1345 after

---

*With a few body parts . . .
**Herons were hot in medieval times. Just trust me on this one.

giving birth to a son, he insisted that Inês become his new bride. Inês and Pedro already had produced several healthy children, whom he thought would make far better heirs than the frail and sickly children mothered by Constanza. But King Alfonso wouldn't hear of it. He insisted Pedro marry royalty, and he banished Inês from court. This, of course, only made the lovers want each other more, and they kept meeting in secret. Eventually King Alfonso had had quite enough of his son's girlfriend, so he ordered Inês's execution. On January 7, 1355, while Pedro was out on a hunt, three assassins rode to the monastery where Inês resided. In front of her children, the assassins chopped off Inês's head with a long sword.* The assassins fled, but in 1361, Pedro captured two of them and ordered their hearts ripped out.**

---

*Well, I warned you this would get tragic.

**He also ate his dinner while the assassins were being executed, because bleeding hearts ripped from chest cavities should never make anyone lose their appetite.

Two years later King Alfonso died, and Pedro was crowned king. Now Pedro needed a new queen, but he had never gotten over his dear, sweet Inês. He also wanted his son from Inês, and not his son from Constanza, to inherit the throne. So Pedro claimed that he had secretly married Inês. Then he got a dispensation from the pope that allowed him to legalize his supposedly secret marriage. Only one problem: Pedro's marriage to Inês did not technically make her a queen. He needed a coronation to accomplish that trick. So he came up with a brilliant solution.

Pedro promised his council he would announce his new queen at her coronation. A throne was placed next to Pedro's throne, and in it a beautiful woman with long blond hair and full regal attire sat with a stiff posture, waiting for her crown. His courtiers filed in. At first none of them could figure out who the woman was, but she smelled a bit like rotten fish. Pedro ordered his subjects to bow and kiss his new queen's hand. When they got a little closer, they realized she looked vaguely familiar. It was Inês . . . or at least what was left of her decaying corpse.*

Inês's tale has gone on to become the Portuguese version of Romeo and Juliet and has inspired art, poetry, and literature. More than twenty operas have been written about these star-crossed lovers. Her fame became so great that when Napoleon's invading French army stumbled

---

*Sure, she was a little rough around the edges, but she still had a certain charm.

upon her tomb in 1811, they broke it open and stole a lock of Inês's yellow hair.*

Pedro died in 1367, and all his scheming to raise his lost love up to a queenly state came to naught. Fernando, the legitimate son born from Constanza, succeeded him as king, and Pedro's actions against Inês's assassins earned him the nickname Peter the Cruel.**

Inês's body did have one very important legacy—she is forever remembered as the corpse that was loved in death as much as she was in life. On her tomb, Pedro inscribed the words that should forever be a reminder of the power of love beyond the grave: *Até o fim do mundo* . . . Until the end of the world. Aww . . . I do love a happy ending.

ATÉ O FIM DO MUNDO...

---

*The hair was later sent as a present to the emperor of Brazil and was lost at sea in 1846.
**History repeated itself with Fernando. In a treaty, he promised to marry Lenora of Castile but backed out of the marriage when he fell in love with the wife of one of his courtiers. This led to a big, old messy war called the 1383–1385 Crisis.

Where are they now?

Pedro's and Inês's bodies are interred in the monastery of Alcobaca in Portugal. The two lovers face each other enclosed in intricately carved white limestone tombs featuring lifelike sculptures of Inês and Pedro surrounded by some seriously mischievous-looking angels. The panel at Pedro's head contains the illustrated scenes of the whole dramatic soap opera. It shows Pedro's departure, Alfonso's council condemning Inês, Inês sent to the executioner, and her ultimate decapitation . . . real cheery stuff. It fails to illustrate her exhumed body and coronation, but that's the kind of thing that is hard to illustrate in limestone.*

*Tiny-print disclaimer: A lot of the evidence from this tale survives from medieval Portuguese chroniclers. These chroniclers are not the most reliable sources, partly because most modern-day historians can't figure out what the heck they were saying. Still, I am a sucker for a good corpse/love story, and I can't have a little thing like dubious sources spoiling my fun.

LOVED TO DEATH

It's been said that absence makes the heart grow fonder. This was especially true with the following love stories.

JUANA OF CASTILE *(1479–1555)* AND PHILIP I *(1478–1506)*

Philip I was so drop-dead gorgeous that Juana of Castile still found him gorgeous after he dropped dead. After Philip's death, she was rumored to have taken her husband's coffin with her on a grand tour across the countryside, repeatedly opening it to kiss his feet.

Some say she was crazy in love. Others say she was just plain crazy. Others think it was all a bunch of lies to make Juana look unfit to rule. Obviously, if Joanie was off her rocker, she couldn't possibly sit on a throne, and that meant her dad, Ferdinand II, could rule in her place. Either way, Juana can't seem to shake the cuckoo reputation and is remembered today as Juana the Mad.

SHAH JAHAN *(1592–1666)* AND MUMTAZ MAHAL *(1593–1631)*

Mumtaz Mahal, the most beloved wife of India's Mughal Emperor Shah Jahan, died after giving birth to her fourteenth child. Shah Jahan was so devastated that he was said to "cry out with grief like an ocean raging with storm." His hair turned gray, and he was forced to use glasses due to his constant weeping. After two years of moping around the palace, he decided on a spectacular way to remember his lost love. A painting? Boring. A lock of hair? Child's play. The world's most elaborately decorated mausoleum that would become one of the seven wonders of the world? Yeah, that will do. The project took approximately twenty-two years to build and more than twenty thousand workers. When Shah Jahan died, his body was placed in a tomb next to his beloved under the large white marble dome. Known today as the Taj Mahal, it is visited by more than two million tourists per year and is one of India's main attractions.

MARIA ELEONORA *(1599–1655)* AND GUSTAV II ADOLF *(1594–1632)*
After the Swedish king Gustav II Adolf died, his wife, Maria Eleonora, just couldn't bear to have him buried in the cold, hard earth. She was rumored to keep his heart in a golden casket above her bed and his coffin next to where she slept . . . with the lid open. Eventually Maria Eleonora agreed to let Gustav be buried, but not before she clung to his body, weeping uncontrollably.

PERCY BYSSHE SHELLEY *(1792–1822)*
AND MARY WOLLSTONECRAFT SHELLEY *(1797–1851)*

Poet Percy Bysshe Shelley once wrote, "Death is the veil which those who live call life." And that was some of his lighter stuff. So we can imagine him feeling a certain macabre delight over what happened to his body in death. First, Shelley checked off all the boxes for a tragic Romantic poet's death. He died young, drowned at sea, and left behind a devastated wife—Mary Wollstonecraft Shelley, the author of *Frankenstein.* When his body was found washed up on the coast of Italy, Italian quarantine laws forbade it to be moved because of fears that corpses spread plague. That meant Shelley had to be cremated right there on the beach. Flames consuming a body as angry waves crashed upon the shore may sound sentimental, but it can get a little creepy when one organ just won't burn. That organ was his heart. His buddy Lord Byron (another tragic poet) was getting so annoyed waiting for the cremation to be done that he just left and went for a swim. Finally his friend Captain Trelawny grabbed the heart from the flames, deciding a poet's heart was not meant to burn.* He kept it for several years and then later gave it to Mary. In 1851, the heart, reduced to dust and wrapped in one of Shelley's poems, was found in Mary's drawer. A fittingly sad end to the poet who also once wrote: "The flower that smiles today/Tomorrow dies."

---

*Some historians claim that it was probably the fatty liver that would not burn, but I am not going to have medical science wrecking my love story.

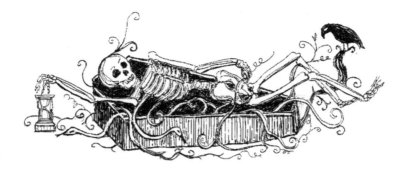

ROSALIA LOMBARDO *(1918–1920)*

The almost-two-year-old Rosalia was so perfectly preserved in a glass casket that she is known today as the Sleeping Beauty. She is stored at the Catacombs of the Capuchin monks in Palermo, Sicily, in southern Italy.

VLADIMIR LENIN, COMMUNIST REVOLUTIONARY *(1870–1924)*

Lenin's body is embalmed and on display in the middle of Moscow's Red Square. The sarcophagus is kept at a constant temperature of sixty-one degrees Fahrenheit, and Lenin's skin is given weekly bleach baths to keep him looking fresh.

EVA PERÓN *(1919–1952)*

Eva's husband, Juan Perón, kept his wife's embalmed corpse in the dining room where he ate. Eva was later interred in the Recoleta Cemetery in Buenos Aires, Argentina.

GALILEO GALILEI

HANGING BY HIS FINGERNAILS

Here is your first lesson on how to collect and trade body parts: don't lose the label! It's just not fair to the person who finds the body part. In 2009 an anonymous seller sold a molar, forefinger, and thumb, never knowing they once belonged to history's most famous astronomer and mathematician. Someone didn't get the full value for those body parts. But Alberto Bruschi, a Florence collector, did. He bought the fingers and tooth at auction for an undisclosed amount. With help from an expert, he later identified them as belonging to Galileo Galilei. He then sold them to Florence's Museum of the History of Science.* The fingers didn't look like anything special. They resembled shriveled-up pieces of beef jerky with fingernails attached. Yet that wizened forefinger had once pointed to the heavens and revealed the universe's secrets.

Galileo did not have an easy time revealing those secrets. In fact, he almost died for them. Part of why he got into so much trouble was his own fault. As a math professor, he had a tendency to state his opinion in an abrasive manner and then treat anyone who contradicted him like an idiot. He was pretty much the scariest math teacher you ever had.

---

*The point of this lesson: there is a profit to be made collecting famous fingers.

In Galileo's defense, math was a tough field back then. At the time, a mathematician made less income than a stonemason. Mathematics was not used like it is today. It was mainly used in astrology to map out the position of the planets in order to predict the future. This meant Galileo's primary job as a mathematician was to cast horoscopes. Astrology just wasn't Galileo's calling.*

Galileo wanted to do more. Much more. He had theories about the universe that went against the Greek philosopher Aristotle's accepted theories. Aristotle was a great guy, but he got a few things wrong. Around 347 BC, Aristotle taught that the earth was at the center of the universe and the sun, moon, and all the other planets revolved around it. Aristotle also believed the stars were perfect celestial bodies created by God and never moved or changed.** More important, the Catholic Church based its teachings about the heavens on Aristotle's writings. No one went against Aristotle's theories. No one except Galileo.

Galileo was armed with something other astronomers didn't possess—a powerful telescope. Of course, it wasn't called a telescope then. It was called a spyglass and was used mostly as a child's toy until Galileo got his hands on one. He started experimenting with grinding lenses, and soon created a telescope that magnified things eight to thirty times more than the toy version, so Galileo could see more than Aristotle had. For example, Aristotle had said the moon had a smooth surface. With his new device, Galileo saw that the moon was filled with valleys, crags, and mountains. It was like telling people that the most beautiful

---

*In one horoscope he cast, he predicted the Grand Duke Ferdinand I would live a long and prosperous life. He died twenty-two days later.

**This meant that everyone got really spooked out when something like a comet went streaking through the sky. Most saw it as a sign that the world was coming to an end.

girl in town secretly had terrible zits. No one wanted to hear that the moon wasn't shiny and perfect.

Then in 1610 Galileo pointed his telescope at Jupiter and discovered four major moons that orbited Jupiter instead of orbiting Earth. He also saw that Venus revolved around the sun, not the earth. If Venus revolved around the sun, was it possible that Earth revolved around the sun too?

This was extremely dangerous thinking. Fifty years earlier, an astronomer named Copernicus had preached that the earth and Venus revolved around the sun, and the Catholic Church had banned his books. Anything that went against the teachings of the Catholic Church was called heresy. Heresy was a very serious accusation that could come with a penalty of death. But this didn't stop Galileo from publishing his findings in a book called *The Starry Messenger*. The book became an instant bestseller and made Galileo famous throughout Europe.

Then Galileo got really cocky. In 1624, he visited Rome to convince the cardinals and the pope the earth revolved around the sun. His friend Cardinal Maffeo Barberini had just been elected pope and took the name Urban VIII. Galileo greatly misjudged Urban's tolerance for new ideas. For one, Urban did not handle disruptions well. He once had all of the Vatican's birds slaughtered because they disturbed his morning slumber. If he had birds killed for annoying him, what would he do to anyone who dared to say the Catholic Church was wrong?

At first Urban said Galileo could continue to write about his findings as long as he did it in the hypothetical. In other words, Galileo was never to state in certain terms that the church was wrong. So Galileo published a book called *The Dialogue*, in which he stated the debate in a narrative between four "hypothetical" people. One of these hypothetical people was a man called Simplicio (meaning "simpleton" or stupid person). In Galileo's book, Simplicio defends Aristotle's Earth-centered beliefs. He also happens to bear an uncanny resemblance to Pope Urban. The book became another bestseller.

When Urban found out he was portrayed as a buffoon in *The Dialogue*, he was not happy. He demanded Galileo come to Rome and stand trial for heresy. Now, here's the funny thing about these sorts of trials: it is very easy to be brazen in the comfort of your home, but when you are faced with impending torture and death . . . your beliefs suddenly change. Galileo recanted everything from *The Dialogue* faster than you can say, "Thumbscrew." He was then put under house arrest, eventually went blind, and died in 1642, probably still ticked off at the pope. One of his students begged to give him a fancy burial, but the church would not allow it. Instead Galileo was buried in the back of the Santa Croce chapel in Florence without much ceremony.

By 1737, the church decided they had been a bit harsh on Galileo and allowed him to be reburied in a fancier marble tomb next to the sixteenth-century artist Michelangelo. During the exhumation, three of the assembled men, Antonio Cocchi, Anton Francesco Gori, and Vincenzio Capponi, couldn't resist stealing some souvenirs before they let Galileo rest in peace. Cocchi helped himself to Galileo's vertebra.

Gori called dibs on Galileo's middle finger from his left hand. Capponi took one of Galileo's molars, along with the very thing that had gotten Galileo in so much trouble—the forefinger and thumb used to write all those troublesome books. These were passed down from generation to generation, and then lost around 1905, until they came up for auction in 2009.

Galileo's vertebra is housed at the University of Padua. Galileo's molar, gnarly thumb, middle finger, and forefinger can be found at Museo Galileo in Florence. The middle finger is enclosed in a gold stand inside an egg-shaped goblet. It points to the heavens that Galileo had once so adored.*

---

*Okay, this is another one of those tiny-print observations that you probably already figured out. Yes, Galileo's middle finger is stuck making a not-so-nice hand gesture for pretty much eternity.

INVASION OF THE
BODY SNATCHERS

Until 1832, it wasn't technically a crime to steal a corpse in Britain. In fact, stealing Grandma's ring off her finger was a felony, but stealing her finger was not. Body snatchers would strip the clothes off a corpse, leave all the possessions in the grave, and then yank the poor soul out of his deep and never-ending sleep.

Stealing bodies was common in Europe and the United States in the eighteenth and nineteenth centuries because medical schools were desperate for corpses to dissect to understand human anatomy. Doctors had previously learned anatomy by dissecting animals like pigs, dogs, and monkeys. This led to some confusion.* Thus, selling corpses to medical schools became a lucrative business for a group of body snatchers called the "resurrectionists." Eventually body snatching became so common that by 1850, six

---

*In the sixteenth century, it was believed that the uterus, the organ where a baby develops, had two demonic horns. This misconception did nothing for the women's movement.

hundred to seven hundred bodies were being stolen yearly from New York graves.

It was not a job for the faint of heart. Medical schools paid only for fresh corpses, so the resurrectionist had to work fast once a body was buried. To deter body snatchers, it became customary for families to wait until their loved one was good and stinkin' dead before burial. In some cemeteries, locked houses called morthouses were used to let bodies decompose for at least three months before burial.

Other families secured iron cages around a coffin or placed heavy stones on top of their loved ones. Probably the most ingenious solution was the torpedo coffin—a coffin with pipe bombs that exploded if disturbed by body snatchers.

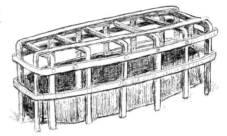

Two of the most notorious body snatchers were William Burke and William Hare. They made a killing supplying fresh corpses to doctor Robert Knox. And I mean literally . . . a killing. Instead of waiting for fresh corpses, they decided to speed things up and just murder people. They murdered sixteen people before they were caught. Hare was released after he gave evidence against Burke. Burke was hanged, and as a rather fitting punishment, his body was used for dissection.

After the dissection, his skin was tanned and made into wallets and books. Legend has it author Charles Dickens owned a bookmark made from Burke's skin.*

*If you share my morbid curiosity, you might be wondering—what exactly does a book made from human skin look like? Well, it actually looks like any other leather-bound book and holds up quite nicely. Really, I promise . . . This book was not made from skin. (Evil laugh . . .)

KING LOUIS XIV

September 5, 1638–September 1, 1715

EAT YOUR HEART OUT

Given how much action King Louis XIV's heart got in life, it is only fitting that his ticker would continue its high jinks in death. Let's just say that Louis had a lot of girlfriends. He was always jumping behind the shrubbery and doing goodness knows what.* He was even rumored to have had an affair with his brother's wife, Henrietta of England, but you know how people just love to talk. It wasn't Louis's fault. Women were drawn to him because he had great hair and played the guitar.** He was also the king, and he never let anyone forget it. He called himself the Sun King because he believed he was the center of the universe.*** Sometimes he thought he was so special that he could heal a deadly disease called scrofula by touching someone. This was called the King's Touch, but today we would just call it "I am pretentious enough to think I am God."

One of Louis XIV's biggest contributions to history was etiquette. Before Louis, people would come over to the palace and trample the lawns, pick all the flowers, throw trash everywhere, and pee in the

---

*Actually, we do know what, but that is beyond the scope of this book.
**Not much has changed.
***Technically, the sun is not the center of the universe. The universe does not have a center because it is infinite. But if anyone had tried to tell Louis this, they would have ended up missing a head.

PLEASE DO NOT PEE IN THE FOUNTAIN.

—LOUIS XIV

fountains (flushing toilets had not been invented). So Louis had the brilliant idea to put up little signs called etiquettes all over the palace grounds to tell people how to behave. The word got passed down into the English language, eventually resulting in a dizzying array of forks.

Sometimes Louis got a little carried away with etiquette. You had to wear the right buttons on your jacket, master the appropriate bow, and sit in a chair correctly (left foot forward). If you dressed right and said the right things, then you got to attend the king's *levée*—that's French for "rising" or "very early morning butt kissing." During the king's levée, you had the honor of watching the king splash water on his face and get dressed.* Louis thought it was all terribly exciting to watch him put on pants. The rest of the court was bored to tears. All this nonsense continued until 1715 when Louis XIV died of a leg infection. He was seventy-six years old, and that was plenty old enough.

We shouldn't be too hard on Louis. He did have his good qualities. To start, he wore fabulous shoes with red heels. If you liked them, though, you were out of luck. Louis decreed that no one could wear red heels except the king. He also built a really fancy palace with a lot of shiny things, called Versailles. It's a great place to go if you ever get food stuck in your teeth. You won't have trouble finding a mirror. Best of all, he waged a ton of battles, and when he needed money to pay for his wars, found some very creative ways to tax the poor.**

*Louis did not bathe. He just splashed some lavender water on his neck, changed his shirt, and was good to go.

**Louis forced the poor to pay taxes on a very essential item—salt. (The nobility were exempt.) Before refrigeration, you either used salt to preserve food or ate rancid meat and risked food poisoning, not to mention possible death.

All of Louis's accomplishments created a solid foundation for the French Revolution. By the 1790s, everyone was pretty tired of kings and queens and the whole messy business of being told what to do by one person. Royals were executed daily, including Louis XIV's descendant, King Louis XVI. The French were entirely efficient about it. They invented a device called the guillotine to chop heads off like a vegetable slicer. No one had to wait in line.

When people got tired of chopping off live heads . . . they turned to the dead ones. In 1793, a group of revolutionaries broke into the tombs inside Saint Denis basilica and played kickball with the skulls. People took all sorts of souvenirs: Henry IV's beard, Saint Denis's head, and Louis XIV's embalmed heart. English nobleman Lord Harcourt later bought Louis XIV's heart and preserved it in a silver casket he would sometimes show to honored guests.

One such honored guest was a geologist and paleontologist named William Buckland. Buckland had made several contributions to paleontology, the study of fossils. In 1824 he was the first to identify and name the Megalosaurus.* In 1829 Buckland also became the first to identify fossilized dinosaur poop, which he named coprolites. While most

paleontologists wouldn't touch dinosaur poop, Buckland wasn't the least bit squeamish. By poking around coprolites and whatever undigested bits might be stuck in it, he proved it contained the clues to what prehistoric animals ate.**

Buckland's interest in diet didn't stop there. He believed his sense of taste could solve life's mysteries. Once, when everyone said St. Paul's Cathedral was leaking saints' blood, Buckland said . . . hogwash. He licked the floor and confirmed what he had expected all along—bat urine.***

With such a curiosity for science, Buckland also made it his mission to taste every animal in the animal kingdom. You know when your mom or dad says, "Eat your peas"? Well, William Buckland preferred more exotic forms of nutrition. He told his kids to eat their earwigs. On special nights, the Bucklands dined on rhinoceros pie, slug soup,

---

*Buckland believed the Megalosaurus was just a giant extinct lizard. In 1842 Richard Owen was the first to identify the Megalosaurus as a separate class of large reptiles called dinosaurs.
**Why no one else had figured this out before Buckland is beyond the scope of this book.
***The legal department wants me to remind you not to lick bat urine . . . not even in the name of science.

mice on toast, grilled porpoise head, hedgehog, kangaroo, stewed mole, barbecued sea slugs, and roast joint of puppy.* His odd culinary tastes made dinner at the Bucklands' an experience few guests would forget. He had a menagerie of exotic pets roaming around his house, including a monkey, a few rare birds, and a hyena. You just never knew when the family pet might end up on the menu.

Lord Harcourt probably did not know about Buckland's eccentric eating habits when he invited him to dinner. After the meal, he brought out the silver casket containing Louis XIV's heart and opened the lid to the shriveled-up specimen. By now it looked more like a piece of dried liver than a heart. This didn't stop Buckland's curiosity. "I have eaten many strange things in my lifetime," he bragged, "but I have never eaten the heart of a king." And before anyone could stop him, Buckland scooped up the heart and gobbled it up.

William Buckland believed you should try everything at least once. Good advice next time you are served liver.**

Where are they now?

William Buckland died shortly after eating Louis XIV's heart and was buried in St. Nicholas's churchyard in Oxfordshire, England. Louis XIV is buried in the Saint Denis basilica, minus his heart.

---

*The stewed mole was not a family favorite, but the earwigs were supposedly quite delicious.

**I am putting this in small print so your parents will miss it, but if they ask you to eat liver, you should flatly refuse. Liver is unabashedly nasty.

BON APPÉTIT! BITES AND BITS

We might think of cannibals as crazed savages wearing few clothes, but eating body parts was once the hoity-toity thing to do. In fact, some people loved eating people parts so much they had a surprisingly hard time choosing which part to ingest. Which would you choose?

JUST A TASTE

Seventeenth-century Italian physician Antonio Maria Valsalva tasted fluids from cadavers to determine how they had died. According to his taste test, gangrenous pus was especially foul and left his tongue "tingling."*

MY ART, MY LIFE . . . MY LUNCH

Mexican muralist Diego Rivera described his work as "My art, my life," but he was also passionate about his food. He especially enjoyed eating fresh cadavers from the morgue. "Women's brains in vinaigrette" was his favorite dish.

IS THAT BONE IN MY BREAD?

When the giant in "Jack and the Beanstalk" yelled, "I'll grind his bones to make my bread," he wasn't kidding. In the 1800s, it was a common practice for bakers to use ground bones to bulk up bread.

---

*Well, duh.

MY MUMMY WRAPPED MY SANDWICH

During the American Civil War, a paper mill owner in Maine named Isaac Augustus Stanwood ran out of rags to make pulp. His solution: he imported ancient mummies from Egypt, stripped the bodies of their wrappings, and used them to make paper. He then sold this special brown paper to butchers and grocers who used it to wrap food and sandwiches.

AZTECS' EASTER FEAST

The Aztecs knew how to honor their handsome young men. No, they didn't make them movie stars or supermodels, but they did worship them like gods. Every year one young male was chosen to impersonate Tezcatlipoca—the god of the night sky. The chosen male would be dressed in fine clothes and given the best food. This would go on for

twenty months until the young Adonis climbed the steps of a one-hundred-foot pyramid, lay down on the altar . . . and waited to have his beating heart ripped out and sacrificed to the gods. The rest of the body was thrown down the side of the temple to be cooked and eaten by the people. Yum.

GEORGE WASHINGTON

February 22, 1732–December 14, 1799

Twenty-Two Years Old
George loses his first tooth.
Others have turned black.

Forty Years Old
George's portrait is painted. He has
had several teeth extracted.

Forty-Nine Years Old
George is fitted for his first
set of false teeth.

Fifty-Seven Years Old
George becomes president.
He has only one tooth left.

STRAIGHT FROM THE HORSE'S MOUTH

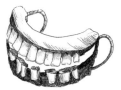

When it comes to George Washington, history tends to repeat the good and leave out the bad. You have probably already heard the good stuff: George Washington was our first president and father of our country, and also a military hero during the Revolutionary War. He threw some great dinner parties, danced a mean minuet (an elegant dance with a lot of twirling), and was said to be the best horseman in the country. He was so honest that after he cut down his father's favorite cherry tree, he immediately confessed to the deed because he "could not tell a lie." One of his biographers made up the cherry-tree story to make George look like a supernice guy. George was a supernice guy, but he also had his share of flaws.

To start, George wasn't always so prim and proper. He could let his powdered hair down once in a while.* He had a terrible temper, and one onlooker said he could curse until "the leaves shook on the tree." Before he married his wife, Martha, he wrote scandalous poetry to his best friend's wife, Sally Fairfax. (She rejected him.) Then there was his darkest, dirtiest secret hidden behind those grandfatherly portraits . . . George Washington's teeth were horrendous.

---

*Yes, that was his real hair. Not a wig.

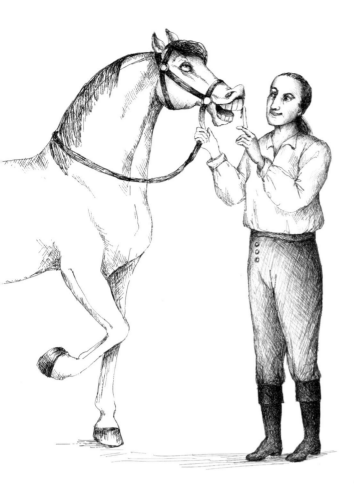

At the age of twenty-two, George had lost his first tooth, while several of his other teeth had turned the color of a rotten banana. He was naturally embarrassed about his bad teeth, so he recorded his dentist bills in his ledger as "hat bills" so people wouldn't know. When people told jokes, he kept his mouth closed, and at dinner parties he ate only soft foods like pickled tripe (cow stomach) because he couldn't chew. All the while, he did his best to keep his teeth clean.

Most people in colonial times didn't bother with teeth cleaning. Dental hygiene was seen as kind of girly, sort of like getting a facial. But George ordered toothbrushes, tooth powders, cloths, scrapers, and sponges. He even made sure his horse's teeth were brushed every day.*

George cheated death many times on the battlefield but was not as lucky cheating malaria, smallpox, and influenza. When he got sick, his doctors prescribed mercury chloride, which had the inconvenient side effect of making his teeth fall out. Like most early colonists, George also had a terrible diet of way too much corn, and he had a fondness for sweets.** People in colonial times did not use toothpaste, but instead

---

*The horse's teeth fared far better.
**Sugared almonds were his favorite.

used tooth powder made from myrrh (a fine powder) or cuttlefish bone. The powders might have cleaned his teeth, but they also scraped the enamel off and caused even more decay. Add to all of this some serious teeth-grinding stress . . . and soon George was losing almost a tooth a year.

Losing a tooth was not as easy as it sounds. Dentists would use a metal instrument called a tooth key to lock on to the tooth and rip it out by the root. (See scary picture.) You can bet this hurt, especially without any anesthesia. The best dentists were quick dentists. Unfortunately, most people could not afford or even find a dentist. At the time of the American Revolution, there were only seventy-nine dentists in the entire country. Some people had their teeth removed by a blacksmith, or even worse, they yanked them out by themselves.

By the time the Revolutionary War hit, George had bullets whizzing by his head and his own secret battle inside his mouth. He had lost so many teeth that he asked his dentist, John Greenwood, to make him some dentures. Dr. Greenwood used cow, elk, donkey, and human teeth attached to a lead base hinged together at the back with metal coils. The human teeth were sometimes George's own teeth or sometimes teeth he bought from his slaves. I know . . . pretty gross. Some dentists even tried to implant teeth from one person into another person. This rarely worked and often led to infection.

George decided to stick with dentures instead of tooth implants, but they were not the sparkly pink-and-white porcelain ones you see today. George's dentures got all brown and icky when the grime and

pickled tripe settled into the cracks. They sort of resembled rotten wood.* Even worse, to keep them in his mouth, George had to constantly clench his jaw and puff out his cheeks. This made him look like a grumpy chipmunk. Still, George hated to complain. In one letter describing his toothache to his dentist, he crossed out the words "give me a great deal of pain" and wrote "are very troublesome to me at times." The British intercepted George's letters about his "troublesome" teeth and had a good laugh.**

By the time George became president, he had only one tooth left, and he was determined to hold on to it. Dr. Greenwood made him another set of dentures with an opening to place over his last tooth. But without any teeth, George's jaw started to collapse, and his cheeks sunk inward. You know that tight-lipped picture of George on the one-dollar bill? When George sat for the original painting by Gilbert Stuart, he stuffed cotton in his mouth to keep his mouth from drooping. That is probably why George looks so pouty on the dollar bill.

By his second term, George not only didn't smile, he didn't speak much. His dentures kept flying out of his mouth, and forming *S-words*

*This is probably how a false rumor started that he had wooden teeth.
**We had the last laugh. We kicked their butt in the Revolutionary War.

caused him a lot of drooling. His second inaugural address was only 135 words—the shortest in history.

When George lost his last tooth in 1796, John Greenwood saved it in a gold-and-glass case that he attached to his pocket watch—a fitting reminder of what time had done to our first president's teeth.

On December 12, 1799, George Washington took to his bed at Mount Vernon after suffering a severe throat infection. His doctors did the usual bloodletting nonsense. They took a scalpel and cut a vein in his arm. Then they let the blood drip, drip, drip into a bowl, like making a fresh pot of coffee.* In George's case, there were a lot of drips—a whopping 3.75 pints of blood. Two days later, George died from a swelling in his airway and also possibly from the blood loss. As usual, he did not complain. His last words were, "'Tis well."

Where are they now?

In 1937, Greenwood's descendants donated George Washington's last tooth to the New York Academy of Medicine. In 1981, a set of George Washington's last remaining dentures was stolen from the Smithsonian in Washington, DC. The bottom dentures have since been found, but not the upper. Another set of dentures can be found at Washington's home in Mount Vernon, Virginia.

---

*Except no one drank it. Promise.

BURIED ... BUT NOT QUITE DEAD

On his deathbed, George Washington made his secretary, Tobias Lear, promise that he would not bury him until two days later. Washington wasn't trying to drag out the mourning. He had a very real fear shared by many in his day—he did not want to be buried alive.

If you think someone alive and kicking couldn't be put six feet under . . . think again. It did happen. Before the invention of the stethoscope, doctors were pretty lousy at detecting death. Sometimes a doctor would stick a dead person's finger into his ear and listen for a buzzing noise. No noise meant no life.

In 1804, in Virginia, Ann Carter Lee was buried alive. She suffered from catalepsy—a condition in which someone passes out and all the muscles in the body go rigid. It's pretty much the best fake death you can possibly pull off. When it happened to Ann, everyone thought for sure she was a goner. So they placed her in a coffin and said their good-byes. A few days later a sexton was bringing flowers and heard a banging noise coming from the coffin. When he opened the lid, Ann sat up, looked around, and was naturally a bit confused as to why she was waking up in a coffin. Her health improved and fifteen months later she gave birth to a baby boy whom you might know. Her son,

Robert E. Lee, would later go on to become one of the most famous Confederate generals in the Civil War.*

Probably the most famous case of being buried alive is the tale of Marjorie McCall. In 1705, in Northern Ireland, Marjorie McCall fell ill and was pronounced dead. The family held a wake for her, and she was buried at Shankill Graveyard. At the time of her burial, she was wearing a valuable ring. Fearing it would attract grave robbers, her family tried desperately to get the ring off her finger, but it would not budge. They were right to be concerned. That night, grave robbers dug up poor Marjorie and tried to steal her ring, but they also could not get it off her finger. So one of the grave robbers got out a knife and began to cut off her finger. Now, falling into a coma and being buried alive really had not fazed Marjorie, but getting her finger cut off . . . well, that got her stirring. The grave robbers were naturally horrified, and they bolted out of the cemetery, screaming. Marjorie lived several more years. Her tombstone bears the inscription, "Lived Once, Buried Twice."

---

*Some historians doubt whether Ann was buried alive, because it was not mentioned in any letters from the Lee family. The story did originate from the Lee family, and in 1934 the details of the premature burial were printed in the *Washington Post*. We will never know for sure, but I am thinking if you accidentally buried a family member, then you might not want to brag about it in letters.

Franz Joseph Haydn

March 31, 1732–May 31, 1809

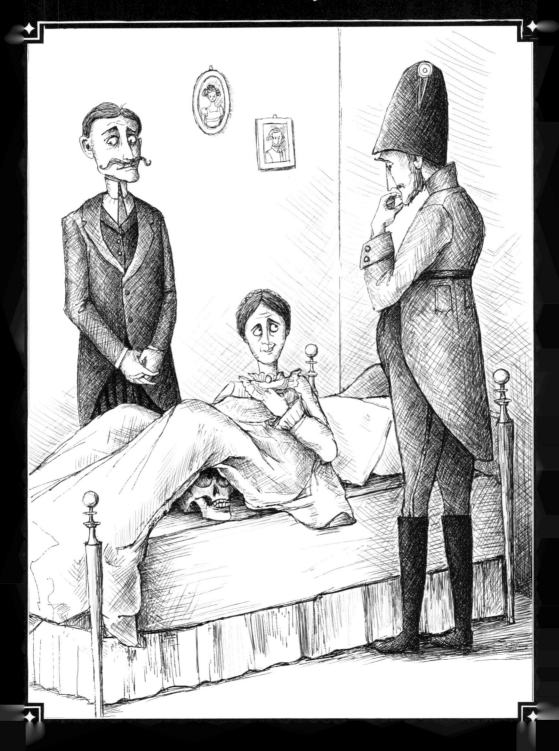

A PIECE OF HIS MIND

If **you are going to steal a head**, it is always best to steal a fresh one, or you are in for an unpleasant job. This didn't stop Joseph Carl Rosenbaum and Johann Nepomuk Peter when they crept into the Hundsturm Cemetery to steal Franz Joseph Haydn's head. It was June 4, 1809, and the corpse had already been in the ground for eight days. It had rotted enough to make Rosenbaum vomit and "it was already quite green," but Rosenbaum was desperate for Haydn's head to aid in his research on phrenology—the hot new brain science.* Phrenologists believed that all those lumps and bumps on your head revealed your personality, sort of like a secret Braille to read someone's character. This spelled trouble if you had one of those funny-shaped heads.** One wrong bump, and you were deemed a deplorable, thieving sot.

Haydn was not some sot. He was a piano composer, mischievous genius, hopeless romantic, and all-around nice guy. He certainly didn't deserve to have his head stolen.

---

*The green yuckiness is a fungus called usnea. It was scraped off criminals' skulls in the seventeenth century and used as a medicine to cure nosebleeds.

**I know a lot of such people with strange-shaped heads, and I assure you that they are positively lovely people who simply don't look good in hats.

On March 31, 1732, Haydn (pronounced "Hi-din") was born in a thatch-covered cottage in the small village of Rohrau, Austria. His childhood was certainly not glitzy, but his mom kept the place clean and little Haydn didn't go hungry. Haydn had an amazing singing voice and exhibited a curiosity for music at a young age. Like any budding rock star, he pretended to play air violin with two sticks until his parents got him some real instruments. By the time he was six, he could play the clavier, violin, and kettledrum. When he was eight, he was sent to Vienna to sing in St. Stephen's choir. St. Stephen's was the glee club of its day. You had to have some serious pipes to make it into St. Stephen's choir. Singers sang for the most important nobility, including Empress Maria Theresa.

Haydn could possibly have grown old and gray singing for his supper if a little thing called puberty hadn't hit. Suddenly hormones were wreaking havoc on his voice, and the empress complained that Haydn was "crowing like a cock." He now had two options. He could do what many young singers did and become a castrato—a castrated male.* Or he could keep his manly voice (and manhood) intact and find a new profession.

He chose to avoid the knife, but it was his mischievous nature that would really be Haydn's undoing. One day he decided to try out a new pair of scissors, and he chopped off the pigtail of a fellow chorister. When the choirmaster found out, he threw Haydn out onto

---

*I am probably going to get into trouble for this one, but since this book is about missing body parts and we are all mature readers, let's take a moment to explain what body part goes missing in a castration. A surgeon cuts off the blood supply to the testicles so they can be removed. Without testicles, the male hormone testosterone is no longer produced, resulting in vocal cords that cannot grow longer. With shorter vocal cords, the singer can continue to hit those high notes. Castration was especially popular with Italian opera singers in the seventeenth and eighteenth centuries. It was made illegal in 1870, when people finally realized that shriveling up an important body part to sing pretty was just sick and twisted.

the streets with only three ragged shirts, a worn coat, and no job prospects. Fortunately, he was given a place to stay by another singer. To earn enough money for food, Haydn serenaded aristocratic ladies in the bitter cold and worked eighteen-hour days teaching students music. Eventually his talents were brought to the attention of Prince Paul Anton Esterházy. The prince gave him a job as an assistant conductor for his orchestra. After the prince's death, Haydn moved to London where he composed some of his greatest works. With old age upon him, he moved back to Vienna, where he became known as the Father of the Symphony. On May 31, 1809, at the age of seventy-seven, Haydn died of old age in his home outside Vienna.

He normally would have had a pretty fancy funeral if he had not croaked at a rather inauspicious time. Emperor Napoleon Bonaparte's army had just beat the snot out of Austria, and French troops were swarming all over Vienna, dropping cannonballs in Haydn's yard. No one was in the mood to honor the dead. The funeral was no-frills, and the burial a hasty affair.

With everyone distracted by the French invasion, it was ridiculously easy to steal a head. Rosenbaum and Peter swiped Haydn's head and then gave it to a group of phrenologists at Vienna General Hospital to be analyzed. These phrenologists boiled, bleached, and scraped off all the fleshy bits so that they could better see the "bump of music" at the skull's temple. It turns out . . . Haydn had a rather big bump there.* After the examination, the phrenologists gave Haydn's freshly scrubbed skull back to Rosenbaum, who kept it in a display case in his home.

Years later, in 1820, the nephew of Haydn's original employer, Prince Nikolaus Esterházy II, decided it was high time to give Haydn a proper burial. So he decided to relocate Haydn's body to a cushy mausoleum to honor the great composer. Now, you can imagine Prince Esterházy's consternation when that copper coffin creaked open, and he found a body, a dashing gray wig, but alas . . . no head. Prince Esterházy was not amused. The police were then tipped off that the skull was at Rosenbaum's house. Fortunately, Rosenbaum got word that the police were on their way, giving his wife time to hop into bed, feign sickness, and hide the skull under her skirts.

Rosenbaum was now in a bit of a pickle. He promised to find that missing head. He had just one problem—you see, he didn't really want to give back Haydn's head. He had grown rather fond of it, as will so often happen when you have a famous composer's skull as part of your decor. So he pawned off another skull as Haydn's head. The ruse worked splendidly. The prince had the anonymous head buried in the fancy mausoleum and was none the wiser.

Until . . . Rosenbaum was on his deathbed and confessed to his doctor that he had done the ole skull switcheroo. Rosenbaum then willed Haydn's head to the Society of the Friends of Music, because that is the right thing to do when you have stolen someone's head. Unfortunately, crooks tend to hang out with other crooks. His doctor

*Well, duh.

38

stole the skull before Rosenbaum could breathe his last breath, and sold it to an Austrian professor. The professor later bequeathed it to the Pathological Museum of the University of Vienna.

By now everyone was tired of playing hot potato with Haydn's head. The Society of the Friends of Music got wind of the missing head and argued that it was the rightful owner, since Rosenbaum had originally bequeathed it to the society. In 1839 the society won the case and placed Haydn's head on a piano where visitors were welcome to study its bumps and rub it like a lucky penny. Haydn would have probably had a good laugh over the hullabaloo. The sense-of-humor bump on his skull was also large.

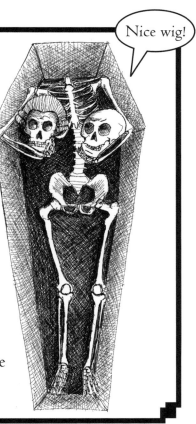

Nice wig!

As years passed, having a famous composer's head on display seemed in seriously bad taste.* In 1954 the Esterházy family convinced the Society of the Friends of Music to reunite Haydn's head with his body. Ironically, Haydn had to share his grave with the original, unidentified skull, because no one had the heart to kick out the extra skull. So two heads, one body, and one fabulous wig now rest in the Bergkirche Church in Austria.

*Especially without a wig on!

PHRENOLOGY—
A BUMPY HISTORY

In the 1790s, Viennese physician Franz Joseph Gall developed craniscopy (later renamed phrenology) to measure a person's character by the bumps on his or her skull. His research was based mostly on observation from the heads around him. For example, he examined a few thieves and noticed that they had a pronounced bump above the ear. Thus, he came to the conclusion that anyone with a raised area above the ear was headed for a life of crime. Dr. Gall also watched Mozart composing music with his knuckle leaning against his temple. This gesture led him to believe that the temple must be the location in the brain where musical skills originated.

Phrenology became extremely popular in the nineteenth century, and soon everyone was sizing up their friends by the shape of their head. Need a job? Your employer would look to see if the top of your head was developed. This indicated a hard worker. Looking for true love? You better hope that you have a large bump at the base of your skull or no one would want to

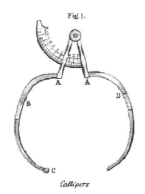

Fig. 1.

Callipers

marry you. Foreheads were especially important in phrenology. If you had a long, high forehead then you were one smart cookie. A low, short forehead meant your IQ was more on par with that of a chimpanzee.*

Gall had good intentions, but his followers did not. Soon every quack was jumping on the phrenology bandwagon and making all sorts of skull-measuring devices. In 1905 the psychograph was invented (shown on the previous page). Looking like a cross between a hair dryer and a medieval torture device, the psychograph used metal rods to measure the skull and then spit out a reading.

Still, phrenology wasn't all malarkey. It did lead to the important discovery that each part of your brain controls a different function. For example, when paleontologists today find a skull, they create an endocast—a mold of the inside of the skull used to determine the size and shape of the brain. If they find two specific enlarged areas called Broca's and Wernicke's areas, that means the owner had evolved toward a higher degree of language skills.

It is from phrenology that we get the term "highbrow," meaning to have sophisticated tastes, and "lowbrow," meaning the opposite—vulgar and uncultured.

---

*Having a short forehead, I would have been deemed a completely vacuous airhead by nineteenth-century standards. This proves beyond a doubt that phrenology was completely bogus.

LUDWIG VAN BEETHOVEN

December 17, 1770–March 26, 1827

SPLITTING HAIRS

If you want to be remembered as a tortured, crazed genius, you better have some serious tortured, crazed hair. Ludwig van Beethoven had a lot of wild rock-star hair and the creepy scowl to match. Fans came out in droves to see the great classical composer on his deathbed. They all wanted the same thing—a lock of his graying hair.* Eventually so many people clipped a strand of Beethoven's hair that he resembled a plucked chicken.

Those who knew Beethoven described him as "utterly untamed." Even as a child, he wouldn't play music like the other kids. He liked to make stuff up instead of following the notes. His dad kept smacking him in the head every time he did this, but it didn't stop Beethoven.

Later in life he could be spotted lumbering through the streets of Vienna like an ape not used to wearing shoes. His clothes were so tattered and dirty that he once got arrested for being a tramp. He laughed too loud, drank too much, and had a bad habit of spitting in people's faces. He was also a hopeless romantic, always falling in love with the wrong person. The object of his affection was usually

---

*People often saved their loved one's hair to weave into jewelry. Google "hair jewelry" and you will find some very beautiful necklaces and bracelets that might just weird you out when you realize that they are made entirely of human hair.

someone above his social station whom he could never marry without your typical Romeo-and-Juliet fallout. It was oh so tragic, but inspired some of his most heart-wrenching piano compositions.*

Beethoven avoided people because people annoyed him. He preferred to be alone, composing music in his underwear . . . much to the chagrin of his neighbors, who sometimes peeked in and got an eyeful. Part of his sour disposition was caused by his equally sour health. He  suffered from terrible stomach pains, eye infections, and kidney stones. But there was a good reason why Beethoven avoided conversations with people—he couldn't hear a word they said. To compose his music, he used an ear trumpet secured with a headband.**

By the time he composed Symphony no. 9, considered one of his greatest works, he was completely deaf. As his health got worse, so did his mood swings. He could be silent and intense one minute, and play practical jokes on his friends the next. When one ardent fan and wife of another composer asked for a lock of his hair, Beethoven sent her some goat's hair. The lady boasted of her memento until she discovered she had been tricked. (Beethoven made up for his prank by later sending her a real lock of his hair.)

---

*Next Internet assignment: google the *Moonlight Sonata* and see if you don't weep like an abandoned baby when you are done listening to it.
**This worked about as well as putting a paper towel roll up to his ear.

Getting a lock of Beethoven's hair was just like asking for an autograph today, so it was only natural that many people would try to swipe a few strands when Beethoven was too weak to protest. One such fan was a fifteen-year-old Jewish boy named Ferdinand Hiller. He and his piano instructor, Johann Nepomuk Hummel, trudged through the snowy streets of Vienna in March 1827 to visit Beethoven before he died. When they got there, they found that Beethoven could barely lift his pale, emaciated limbs, and his stomach had swollen up with so much fluid that he looked like he was about to give birth to a baby elephant. He was suffering from a whole array of illnesses: dropsy, liver failure, pneumonia . . . take your pick. Beethoven was a mess. After he'd spent hours and hours writhing in pain, a thunderstorm clapped above his head. Suddenly Beethoven raised his fist to the skies to utter his last words—"Applaud, friends, the comedy is finished."

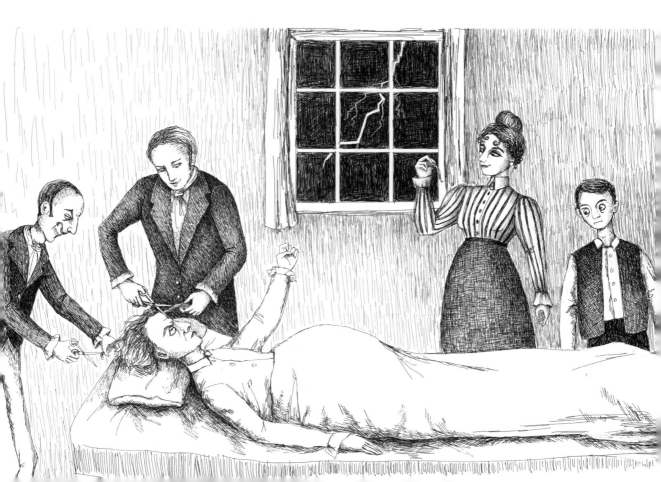

But the real drama was just getting started, and it was to follow Beethoven's hair. The hair that Ferdinand Hiller had cut was passed down to his son, Paul Hiller, who kept it in a dark wooden-frame locket between two sheets of glass. Paul Hiller died in 1934, just before his friends and family were tortured by the Nazi regime. At the time, Jews could not vote or own property, and many were sent to concentration camps, where they never made it out alive. Many Jewish people would hide their most precious items on their bodies when they tried to escape to neutral countries.

The trail of Beethoven's hair grows cold during these years, until October 1943, where it reappeared in a church in Gilleleje, Denmark. There, hidden in the attic of a red-tiled-roof church, a Jewish refugee grasped the locket containing Beethoven's hair in the palm of his hand. Like the other eighty refugees he sat huddled next to, he was praying the boats would arrive soon to help him escape to war-neutral Sweden. This refugee's prayers were never answered, and his name is lost to history, but his last act before Nazi soldiers broke down the doors of the church was an important one—he passed the locket along to the man who was helping him hide, Dr. Kay Flemming.

Flash forward to 1994. The locket then came up at auction where Beethoven enthusiasts purchased it. The collectors had always wanted to own a piece of Beethoven, and now they could use DNA testing to reveal how Beethoven suffered in his final years. What testing revealed about Beethoven's hair startled everyone . . . Beethoven had been poisoned. But it wasn't your typical poison-in-your-goblet type of poisoning. Nope. Not nearly as cool. Beethoven was poisoned by a substance in his environment—lead. During his life, lead was in everything. It was used to line eating utensils and to sweeten wines.* Sometimes lead was

---

*Beethoven drank a lot of wine.

brushed on bakery goods to make them glow or it was mixed into mustard and cheese to give them that extra sparkle. On top of the usual lead exposure, Beethoven's doctors also prescribed lead-lined pills to treat his

lead-lined

lead

more lead

lead

lead for sparkle

deafness. By the time of his death, Beethoven's hair contained forty-two times the amount of lead found in normal hair. The symptoms of lead poisoning can lead to all sorts of nastiness—abdominal pains, mood swings, and even hearing loss.

Before he died, Beethoven had written the following request: "As soon as I am dead, if Dr. Schmidt is still alive, ask him in my name to describe my malady . . . so that so far as it is possible at least the world may become reconciled to me after my death." Through the powers of science, Beethoven finally got his wish.

Where are they now?

Locks of Beethoven's hair can be found at the Library of Congress in Washington, DC, the British Library in London, and the Beethoven-Haus in Bonn, Germany.

SOME HAIRY HISTORY

Two hundred years ago, when someone famous came to town, no one asked for an autograph; they asked to take a snip of hair.* When two people liked each other, they did not become Facebook friends; they sent each other locks of hair. And when a loved one died, they didn't reminisce over pictures; they remembered them through their strands of hair pressed into frames and lockets. Today we can use hair to learn a lot about people—just one hair follicle contains a person's DNA and can reveal secrets about health and personality.

EDGAR ALLAN POE *(1809–1849)*

Poe's hair may have always been neat, but his body was a wreck. On October 3, 1849, the poet and author was found delirious outside a tavern, wearing someone else's clothes. He was taken to a nearby hospital, where he died four days later. Historians have long suspected rabies as the cause of his death, but his hair revealed another problem—Poe had arsenic poisoning. In 2006 hair testing found fifteen times the normal levels of arsenic. Historians believe he most likely ingested it through the drinking water. Although the levels weren't high enough to kill him, arsenic poisoning would have led to such nastiness as confusion, vomiting, headaches, and ironically . . . hair loss.

---

*Note to adoring fans: it is entirely okay to ask me for my hair instead of an autograph.

CHARLES DARWIN *(1809–1882)*

Poor Darwin. Throughout his life, the naturalist suffered from vomiting, stomach pains, flatulence, daily diarrhea, and constant fatigue. He had such bad health that his doctors eventually just thought he was making it all up. In 2013 a research team tested two hair follicles from Darwin's beard. What they found astonished everyone. Darwin had Crohn's disease—an inflammatory bowel disease. It didn't kill him (a heart attack did that), but it  sure must have made for some interesting runs to the bathroom on the HMS *Beagle*.* His hair also contained the genes associated with enhanced memory, risk taking, and baldness.

ELVIS PRESLEY *(1935–1977)*

We can't choose how we are going to die, but some of us have more options than others. Aside from Elvis's gastrointestinal and drug problems (see p. 136), his hair also revealed that he had a rare genetic heart disease called hypertrophic cardiomyopathy. This disease causes the heart to become abnormally thick, and if left untreated, will eventually lead to death. His hair also contained the genes associated with glaucoma, migraines, and obesity—all problems Elvis experienced in his lifetime.

---

*Darwin spent eighteen months of his five-year trip to collect specimens stuck on a royal navy ship. Bathrooms consisted of a hole in a plank on the upper deck and had no privacy.

ABRAHAM LINCOLN

February 12, 1809–April 15, 1865

FROM THE CRADLE
TO THE GRAVE
(And Another Grave . . . And Another Grave)

A few days before April 14, 1865, President Abraham Lincoln had a bizarre dream. He was in the East Room of the White House, where a large crowd had gathered beneath the room's ornate crystal chandelier. Heads were lowered in prayer. The only sound was the shuffling of feet kicking up dust from the faded rug. He pushed his way through the throng of people. As he got closer and closer, he realized there was something in the center of the room. It was a corpse. Lincoln turned to one of the mourners and asked who had died. The mourner replied, "The president. He was killed by an assassin."

On April 14, 1865, that dream came true when John Wilkes Booth (p. 76) shot President Lincoln during a play at Ford's Theatre. Lincoln died the next day. Did Lincoln predict his own death? Perhaps. But it didn't take a psychic to know that his life was in danger. After his unpopular decision to emancipate slaves, along with the deaths of 620,000 soldiers during the Civil War, Lincoln had numerous death threats. With so many plots to kill him, it is no wonder that his body would continue to get its fair share of action even after his death.

The first step in his afterlife adventure began just as he had dreamed—his embalmed body was laid out in the East Room. Then

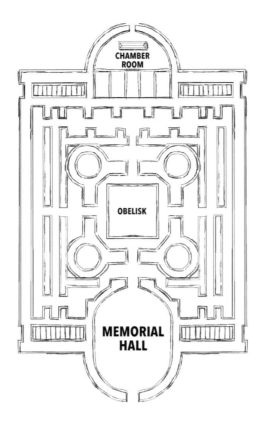

CHAMBER
ROOM

OBELISK

MEMORIAL
HALL

Lincoln's funeral train traveled through 180 cities in seven states. Nearly every city that greeted him shrouded their buildings in black bunting. Funeral dirges played, and church bells rang out. Lincoln was then placed in a temporary tomb in Oak Ridge Cemetery in Springfield, Illinois, while his more posh tomb was being built. When it was finished in 1871, Lincoln was placed in a white Italian marble sarcophagus in the main chamber room. (See diagram above.)

After all this moving around, Lincoln should have rested in peace. Such was not the case. The trouble actually began hours before Lincoln's assassination. At eleven a.m. on April 14, 1865, Secretary of Treasury Hugh McCulloch burst into Lincoln's office and warned the president that they had a serious problem. The crime of counterfeiting, or making fake money, was out of control. Counterfeit rings were growing at such an alarming rate that half the currency in the North was fake. If people didn't trust money, then they wouldn't use it, and the whole economy would collapse. McCulloch's solution was to form a permanent organization of government officials to arrest counterfeiters.

Three months later the Secret Service was created. You know those men in the crisp suits, dark sunglasses, and very serious expressions

Engraving Tools

always hanging around the president? Well, that wasn't this Secret Service. At least not yet. The Secret Service's job was to go after counterfeiters, otherwise known as coney men.*

One of the most talented counterfeiters was an engraver named Benjamin Boyd. His specialty was a five-dollar bill so perfect it fooled even experts. Boyd had a good run until October 21, 1875, when the Secret Service caught and arrested him. Boyd was given a ten-year prison sentence.

Boyd's arrest became a huge problem for a Chicago crime boss named Jim Kennally, otherwise known as Big Jim. Big Jim worked as a middleman selling counterfeit money for half the price. Now with Boyd gone, the quality of counterfeit money went downhill. Criminals were not willing to pay what they had before, and that hurt Big Jim's business. He needed his top counterfeiter back.

That was when Big Jim came up with a plan. A kidnapping plan. But

---

*It was not until President William McKinley was assassinated in 1901 that the government realized the president was going to need more than a couple of bodyguards to protect him from nut bags. The Secret Service got the job.

Terrence Mullen   John Hughes   Lewis Swegles

instead of kidnapping a live person and holding him for ransom, he would kidnap a corpse. And he would kidnap none other than Abraham Lincoln's corpse. He would then agree to return Lincoln's body in exchange for Boyd's release and two hundred thousand dollars.

It sounds crazy, but the scheme was not going to be that hard to pull off. To start, no night watchmen protected Lincoln's tomb. In fact, the only thing standing in the way of a thief and Lincoln's body was a padlock on a wooden door. All Big Jim needed was the right men to carry out his diabolical plan. He chose Terrence Mullen, a bowlegged, stocky man who kept a pet snake in a box and always had a pistol on his belt that he was not afraid to use. The second guy in charge was John Hughes, a sharp dresser with a thick, wiry beard and a long reputation as a counterfeiter. The third guy was probably not the best choice. He was Lewis Swegles, a baby-faced twenty-year-old who always had some unbelievable story to tell of his life running from the law. He convinced Hughes and Mullen that he was the "boss body snatcher of Chicago." Swegles was really the boss "roper," or paid informant, for the Secret Service. He was originally just trying to gather information on Hughes's and Mullen's counterfeiting operations. He uncovered a much bigger plot.

When Swegles told the Secret Service of the body-snatching scheme, they decided the only way to get evidence against the thieves was to arrest them in the act of stealing Lincoln's body. So on November 7, 1876, Secret Service agents hid in the front vestibule area of the tomb, ready to catch the thieves.

Meanwhile, Mullen and Hughes sawed off the padlock on Lincoln's tomb, cut open the end of the marble sarcophagus, and yanked out the lead-lined cedar coffin. Unfortunately, they had not anticipated Lincoln's coffin to be so darn heavy (about five hundred pounds). So Mullen asked Swegles to go outside and get their accomplice to bring around the wagon. But instead of getting the wagon, Swegles gave the code word to arrest Mullen and Hughes. Seconds later shots rang out. One of the Secret Service men's guns had accidentally fired. Tipped off, Mullen and Hughes ran into the woods and avoided capture.

With the thieves on the loose, the custodian of the Lincoln Monument, John Carroll Power, worried that they would try to steal Lincoln's body again. So he and a few trusted men dragged the very heavy coffin out of its marble sarcophagus and decided to put Lincoln where no one would look for him—in a hole in the monument's filthy basement. Unfortunately, when he started to dig the hole, he hit water. He couldn't stick Lincoln's coffin in muddy water. So instead he just threw some moldy lumber on top of it to make it look like a junk pile.*

As for Mullen and Hughes, they were eventually arrested a few months later and each served a one-year sentence. The sentence was short because the Secret Service never really caught them in the act and body snatching wasn't a crime yet in America. (See p. 16 on body snatching.)

Two years later Power felt a tad guilty that our most beloved president sat in a pile of rubbish in a dank, dark basement. So he and a few men dug another hole in the basement where the water was not so high. And yet again . . . Lincoln was moved into another grave. (Still in the basement, but at least belowground.) They then formed a secret group called the Lincoln Guard of Honor and swore never to tell where Lincoln was buried. In 1887 (probably still feeling guilty) they moved Lincoln's body out of the basement and into an unmarked location under the floor of the tomb's chamber.**

Years passed, and rumors spread that Lincoln was not in his fancy marble sarcophagus. In 1901 the Lincoln Guard of Honor (probably still feeling guilty) decided they needed a safer place for the body. Once again Lincoln's body was moved. Of course, they couldn't resist

---

*Because moldy lumber is far nicer than muddy water.

**By now you are probably losing count of the moves. Some historians count Lincoln's body as moving seventeen times, but many of those moves were temporary moves that occurred on the same day. Let's just say for the sake of argument that he was moved *a lot*.

taking a peek inside to make sure he was still there. The coffin was cut open and . . . sure enough, Abe was still there. He looked "somewhat shrunken" and a bit brown, had hair sticking up "like a horse's," but otherwise was not too shabby for a thirty-six-year-old corpse. Lincoln was then put ten feet below the monument's floor, encased in a steel cage, and sealed in solid concrete. And that is where Lincoln remains today. Hopefully, he is done moving.

Where are they now?

The bodies of Lincoln, his wife, and his three youngest sons lie beneath a 117-foot-high granite obelisk in Oak Ridge Cemetery located in Springfield, Illinois. The grandiose structure is called the Lincoln Tomb, and the cemetery is the second-most visited cemetery in the country. If you walk to one side of the Lincoln Tomb, you will find a giant dark bronze face of Lincoln. The first thing you will notice is that Lincoln looks like he is wearing sun block on his nose. The golden-colored nose happened over time from people rubbing it for good luck.

PICKLING PICKS

People have done all sorts of things to keep corpses from turning green and smelly. Here are a few of the most successful.

LET'S STAY TOGETHER

The ancient Egyptians get all the credit for making some fabulous mummies, but the Chinchorro people of northern Chile and southern Peru were mummifying bodies two thousand years before the Egyptians. They treated the body like a jigsaw puzzle—they broke it apart and then put it back together. First they stripped off all the skin and tanned it in the heat. Then they pulled apart all the bones and preserved them in white ash. When all the bits were saved, they reassembled the bones by reinforcing the skeleton with sticks, and then reapplied the skin using clay and black manganese.

SWEET ON DEATH

Alexander the Great left specific instructions to stick his corpse in a vat of honey after his death. Alexander held up pretty well. His corpse was displayed in a glass coffin for decades, and everyone said he looked lifelike. Honey does do a splendid job preserving a body. Its high sugar content draws out the water, turning the body into sweet beef jerky.

I'LL DRINK TO THAT

After his death at sea in 1805, British Vice Admiral Lord Horatio Nelson was preserved in a cask of brandy until his body could be brought on land. Oddly, there was a lot less brandy once the crew reached the shore. It was rumored that some of his soldiers took a few swigs of Nelson's brandy bath on the way home. More likely, the body absorbed the brandy, making it seem like there was less.

FROZEN IN TIME

In 1865 Lincoln's body was embalmed—a process to preserve the body to prevent decomposition. To embalm Lincoln's body, doctors made an incision in Lincoln's femoral artery, in the right upper thigh, and then pumped in zinc chloride. The zinc chloride gave the skin a spooky glow and froze Lincoln's features like a marble statue.

Before 1840, when soldiers died on the battlefield, they were placed in wood or metal coffins filled with ice and transported by wagon. It made for a smelly ride (especially in the heat). That changed after the Civil War. One out of every four soldiers did not return home alive, and that added up to a lot of bodies needing to be shipped home for burial (620,000 to be exact). Seeing a business opportunity, embalmers would follow the army from battle to battle and set up tents on the battlefield to offer their services. Family members could claim their loved ones and then bring the body over to the embalming tent to get spruced up.

STUCK ON YOU

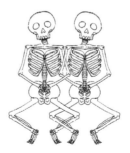

This is the story of two brothers who did everything together. They slept together, ate together, played together, and even went to the bathroom together. Chang and Eng Bunker had the kind of brotherly bond that could never be severed. I mean, seriously . . . no one could break them apart. Chang and Eng were stuck together.

They were born in 1811 on a bamboo mat in a thatch-roof house floating on a river near Bangkok, Siam (modern-day Thailand). A two-inch-thick band of flesh connected the brothers at their abdomens, forcing them to coordinate their four legs and four arms like two dancers caught in a never-ending waltz. They could run together, swim together, and even row a boat in unison.

When they were kids, doctors gave their mother some interesting suggestions on how they could be separated. One said to use a red-hot wire, while another suggested using termites to eat away at the connecting flesh. Another doctor suggested hanging the boys from their connected skin across a catgut cord like laundry airing out to dry. Supposedly, this would stretch and sever the bond. Luckily, Chang and Eng's mom had the good sense not to listen to the boys' doctors.

When Chang and Eng were thirteen years old, they met American

trader Abel Coffin.* Coffin immediately saw that a fortune could be made off Chang and Eng. Before YouTube videos and reality TV, America was hungry for "freak shows."** Dwarfs, giants, bearded ladies, and any person whose deformity made them different were put on public display and could be viewed for a price. Conjoined twins were extremely rare. Even today, only one in about fifty thousand births are conjoined, and the survival rate is only up to 25 percent. Coffin knew Chang and Eng would attract crowds, so he purchased the boys from their mother for three thousand dollars—enough to support her for life. They then boarded a ship to Boston to start a whirlwind tour in America.

They are known today as conjoined twins, but the show posters called them the Siamese Double Boys, after their birthplace of Siam.*** Medical professionals were amazed by the twins, and they performed

---

*Yes, I get a little giddy when I find people with names associated with death.
**Calling someone a freak today is just not cool, and many states have banned shows that exploit the disabled.
***It is from Chang and Eng that we get the term Siamese Twins.

all sorts of scientific experiments to see how their bodies worked. In one of these tests a doctor fed Chang asparagus but did not give any to Eng. Four hours later he took a good whiff of both twins' urine. Chang's urine had that very pungent curl-your-nose-hairs smell. Eng's urine did not.* This experiment told the doctor that they did not share a urinary tract. Naturally, many medical professionals wondered if they could separate the twins, but most thought it was far too dangerous. Most likely Chang and Eng would not have survived such a surgery. Before the discovery of antibiotics, you could get a small cut and die if it became infected.

When Chang and Eng reached their majority at the age of twenty-one, they were sick of being gawked at and wanted to lead a normal life. They quit touring and took the last name of Bunker. With enough savings from their shows, they built a wooden house in Mount Airy, North Carolina, high on a sloping hill with oversize windows to let in the light. They even found true love when they met two sisters—Sarah Anne and Adelaide Yates. Chang and Eng both fell for Adelaide, but it was Chang who won her heart and asked her to marry him. Her sister, Sarah Anne, later agreed to marry Eng.** It may seem strange to choose one twin over the other, but the brothers had two completely different personalities. Eng was the nice guy—he was easygoing and intellectual. Chang was the bad boy—he was witty but also angered easily and was a bit of a drunk.

Despite their differences, the twins got along enough to have twenty-one children with their two wives.*** They lived in two houses where they would spend three days in one house and then three days in the

---

*What does asparagus urine smell like? Now, let's not be lazy. Go eat some and get back to me.
**This might not count as a love triangle.
***Some reports state that they had twenty-two children. One starts to lose count after twenty-one.

other. They also became successful businessmen, selling tobacco and farming the land. Despite having to share a body, the twins had pretty normal lives.

Then the Civil War broke out and, like most people in the South, they were financially ruined. Without means to support their families, Chang and Eng were forced to go back to touring as curiosities. They teamed up with P. T. Barnum, one of the greatest showmen of his day.

But Chang's drinking started to take its toll, and on one return trip home, he had a stroke. From then on, Eng was forced to use a leather strap to hold Chang up like a floppy puppet. Chang's health deteriorated until one day he got bronchitis. The next morning, Eng awoke to find his brother's skin cold to the touch. Chang had died in his sleep. Eng immediately knew his life was in danger and sent for the doctor. But this was the days of horse and buggy . . . not an ambulance in sight. By the time the doctor got to the house, Eng was dead too. The twins were sixty-two years old.

If Chang and Eng were worth something alive, they sure as heck were worth something dead. Immediately offers started to come in to purchase the bodies. One was as high as ten thousand dollars—a small fortune then. Sarah Anne and Adelaide refused, but became worried that body snatchers would steal the bodies. So they buried the twins in the floor of their basement, where no one could get at them.

After the twins' deaths, a Philadelphia doctor named Dr. William Pancoast convinced the sisters to allow an autopsy. The autopsy revealed something interesting about their liver—it was also conjoined. You just don't find a conjoined liver every day, so of course, Dr. Pancoast was not about to give it back. He stole the liver, along with some token intestines. He then sewed the twins back up, took a really creepy plaster cast of their bodies, and sent the corpses home to their widows. The sisters never noticed the missing bits and reburied the twins in the basement.

Today the Bunkers have more than fifteen hundred descendants. Every year about two hundred of them get together for one raucous family reunion where they wear T-shirts that read, OUR FAMILY STICKS TOGETHER. Chang and Eng certainly did stick together. Keep that in mind the next time you want to pummel your brother or sister.

Where are they now?

The twins were later reburied in the cemetery of White Plains Baptist Church in North Carolina. Chang and Eng's liver, along with their plaster cast, can be viewed at the Mütter Museum in Philadelphia.

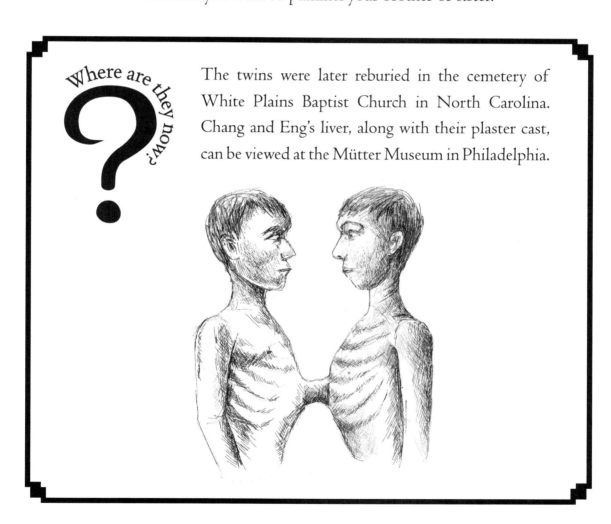

IT'S FUN TO SHARE

You do not have to be a conjoined twin to share body parts. Here are some of the most common parts used in tissue and organ transplants.

Head: Yes, a head transplant is possible. *Read the following page . . .*

Corneas: The cornea is the outermost layer of the eye. Donating your corneas helps people see again.

Temporal Bones: The temporal bones are the bones located on either side of the skull. These are used to help deaf people hear again.

Heart and Liver: Hearts and livers are donated from a beating-heart cadaver—a person whose brain is dead but heart is still beating.

Kidney: A kidney may be donated from a living or dead person, but organ transplants from living donors are more successful.

Blood: About one in seven people entering a hospital needs blood. The most valuable blood type is O negative. People with type O negative are universal donors and can give blood in an emergency when the needed blood type is unknown. And, no, you don't have to be alive to give blood. Cadaver blood can be used.

Bones: Can be used in dental implants. They also can be made into screws and plates to be used to repair a broken leg.

Skin: Skin is removed and grafted onto a burn victim. This prevents burn victims from losing heat and water.

TWO HEADS ARE BETTER THAN ONE

When you think of organ transplants, a head transplant probably doesn't come to mind.* Yet it has been done. On May 21, 1908, Charles Guthrie attached one dog's head upside down to another dog's neck.** Although the two dogs did not survive the operation, Guthrie was able to get the blood of the intact dog to flow to the decapitated dog's head and back again to the intact dog. It may sound like something out of a horror movie, but science is not too far off from making this a reality. In 1970 Robert White successfully transplanted one monkey head onto another monkey head. White claimed head transplants would lead to breakthroughs in organ transplant. Other scientists called the experiments "bizarre" and "worthless."***

*Unless you have my demented mind.
**And, yes, there is a photo of the experiment. Just google it.
***It also may result in a demand for two-headed pets.

PHINEAS GAGE

1823–May 21, 1860

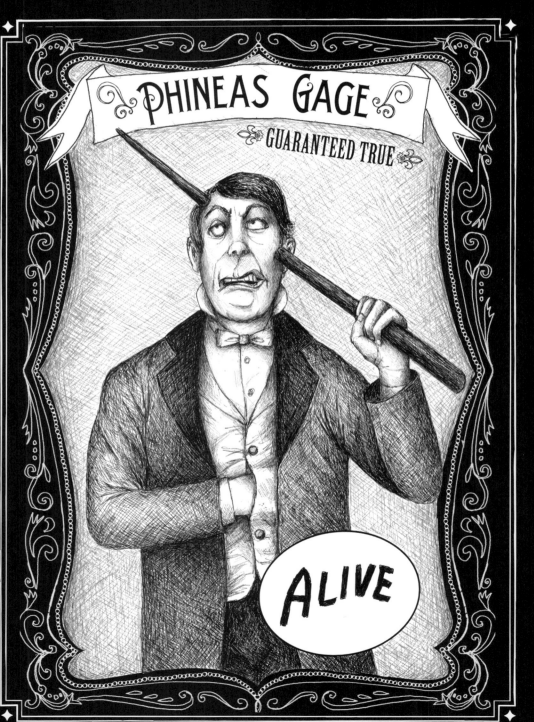

A HOLE IN ONE

Would you pay ten cents to see a pulsating brain inside a man's skull? Many people in the nineteenth century did. It was hard not to be curious when they saw the poster at P. T. Barnum's American Museum: THE ONLY LIVING MAN WITH A HOLE IN THE TOP OF HIS HEAD. The illustration depicted a burly man named Phineas Gage with a long metal pole lodged right through his head. Like most circus posters, not all the details were true. But the hole at the top of Phineas Gage's skull was very real, and it should have killed him.*

It was four thirty on September 13, 1848. Dust swirled around the granite rock bed that was being cleared to build a railroad through Cavendish, Vermont. Phineas Gage, the railroad foreman, squinted his eyes at the afternoon sun and shuffled his long forty-three-inch tamping iron pole along the ground like a baseball player waiting for his turn to bat. The tamping iron pole was 1.25 inches at its thickest point and had a blunt end to pack down sand. The railroad worker's job was to dig a hole in the granite, fill it with explosives, and then cover it with sand. The sand was the important part. It kept the

---

*This book probably should have had this disclaimer on the first page, but here goes: if you are squeamish . . . do not read on.

explosives from going off at the wrong time. Unfortunately, on that day, someone got stingy with the sand.

Gage pounded his tamping iron into a hole, just like he had done a thousand times before. A spark ignited. Boom! The tamping iron flew out of his hand, went through his cheek, out the top of his skull, and landed roughly twenty-five feet away with part of his brain still stuck to the end.*

Gage fell onto his back, his face a horror show of blood. Most of his friends just assumed he was a goner, but Gage sat up and started to speak. The men helped Gage into an ox cart and took him home to see a doctor.

About an hour later Dr. John Martyn Harlow arrived. Although Gage was bleeding from his mouth, cheek, and skull, he acted like nothing had happened. In fact, he even sent visitors away because he planned to be back to work the next day.

This doesn't hurt a bit!

Dr. Harlow was not so convinced. He thrust one index finger into the top of Gage's skull and his other index finger into the wound at Gage's cheek until the two fingers met.** The tamping iron had made a complete hole in Gage's skull. Dr. Harlow didn't know what to do. No one could possibly survive such an injury. He did the best he could to treat Gage's wound. He cleaned out the bits of bone fragments

*This is your last warning. This is going to get gory.
**He most likely didn't wash his hands before examining Gage. At the time, doctors had no clue that sticking fingers into an open wound could introduce harmful bacteria that could lead to life-threatening infection.

70

from the skull, pulled the loose skin back into place with adhesive tape, and placed Gage's nightcap over his broken skull. Dr. Harlow then bled Gage by cutting a vein in his arm and letting some of the blood drip into a bowl.* Then Dr. Harlow prescribed a purge—herbs to make Gage vomit. The purge caused Gage to eject a "teacupful of brains."**

I love my rocks.

Fourteen days later "a fungus" sprouted out of Gage's skull and he developed a high fever. At this point his family measured him for a coffin and said their good-byes. But surprisingly, Gage got better. Unfortunately, having a hole in his head did not improve his personality. Before the accident, Gage had been a docile, well-liked, easygoing guy. The post-accident Phineas Gage was a real jerk. Gage's friends said he was irritable, used foul language, and was so changed that he was "no longer Gage." He also had some comprehension problems. To test Gage's reasoning skills, Harlow offered Gage one thousand dollars for some pebbles that Gage had collected along the riverbank. Gage refused. He clearly either really, really liked his pebbles or had become a tad nutty.

Because of his altered personality, the railroad refused to hire him

*It may sound barbaric, but bleeding actually may have helped Gage get better. When a brain is injured, it swells and needs room to expand. If it does not have room to expand, oxygen can be cut off to the rest of the body. Drawing blood reduces blood pressure and may have taken some pressure off Gage's brain.
**A "teacupful" of brain would be about one quarter cup and would not be taken with sugar.

I love
my rod . . .

back. So Gage found work next to bearded ladies and Siamese twins in P. T. Barnum's American Museum in New York City, where he displayed his head wound along with his tamping iron. (But, no, the tamping iron was not stuck in his head like the poster illustrated.) Gage took that tamping iron with him from job to job. He took it with him when he worked in a livery stable in New Hampshire for ten months, and he took it with him when he worked as a stagecoach driver in Chile.

Due to his injury, Gage's health continued to fail until he was forced to move back to San Francisco to be cared for by his family. While in San Francisco, he had a series of seizures. A seizure is abnormal electrical activity inside the brain. Every brain contains one hundred billion nerve cells called neurons. Neurons transmit signals in the brain like wires in a computer. Some people may experience seizures from having too many or too few neurons firing at the same time. In Gage's case, his seizures were caused by damaged neurons. In 1860 Gage died after a long seizure. Despite a big hole in his head, he had survived eleven and a half years after his injury.

Today Gage has become one of the most popular case studies for scientists to understand how brain damage can alter someone's personality. The part of the brain that was damaged in Gage's case was his left frontal lobe. Remember the phrenologists from page 40? Well, nineteenth-century doctors believed the reason Gage's personality was altered was because his "Organ of Benevolence (Kindness)" bump was damaged. Scientists today know that measuring the bumps on someone's skull means very little, but different parts of the brain do control different thought processes. In Gage's case, the damage to his left frontal lobe impaired his emotional reasoning and his ability to make decisions.

Dr. Harlow continued to be curious about Gage's brain, even after Gage's death. In 1867 he wrote to Gage's mother and asked her if she wouldn't mind digging up her son and sending along his skull. Mrs. Gage did one better. She not only sent Dr. Harlow her son's skull, but also the tamping iron that had been buried in Gage's casket. Today we are thankful Gage's mom was so generous, because it has allowed scientists to study one very cool way to cheat death.*

Where are they now?

Gage's skull and tamping iron can be viewed at the Warren Anatomical Museum in the Harvard University School of Medicine in Massachusetts. They are not part of public display, so you must ask nicely to see them. The skull looks like a normal skull, if it were not for the irregular, triangular-shaped hole at the top.

---

*Also impressive is that you made it to the end of this chapter. Congratulations! Time for lunch.

BURY THE HATCHET
AND THEN SOME

Phineas Gage's rod may seem like an odd thing to bury with him, but people have buried all sorts of wacky things with their loved ones.

EVERYTHING BUT THE KITCHEN SINK

The Ancient Egyptians never packed lightly for the afterlife. They buried their dead with cosmetics, clothes, tools, food, jewels, and furniture. But probably the strangest thing that they buried with their dead was the family pet. Many tombs contained mummified monkeys, elephants, lions, donkeys, dogs, and of course the most sacred of all the Egyptian pets—cats.

EAT YOUR WORDS

In 1862 poet and painter Dante Gabriel Rossetti laid to rest his beautiful wife, Elizabeth Siddal. Utterly heartbroken and clearly needing to make a melodramatic gesture, Rossetti buried his poems entwined in Elizabeth's red hair. This seemed like a good idea at the time except . . . he forgot to make copies. Years later Rossetti's agent, Charles Augustus Howell, dug up poor Lizzie to retrieve his client's poems.* Unfortunately, a worm had burrowed through the poems, leaving a big wormhole.

---

*Because a good agent will do that.

WHEN YOU'VE GOT TO GO . . .

It has to be the most important question for those journeying into the afterlife—where to go to the bathroom? If you were an emperor buried during the Han Dynasty (206 BC to AD 220), then no worries. The Han Royal tombs were buried with everyday items such as tools, food, weapons, furniture, and even stone toilets.

SMELLING LIKE ROSES

Pop artist Andy Warhol (1928–1987) could be a little vain. He had a nose job and dyed his hair silver so that his face would always look young. He also loved perfume and once said, "Another way to take up more space is with perfume." Knowing his need to smell pretty, his loved ones buried him with a bottle of Estée Lauder Beautiful.

PRINCE OF DARKNESS

Actor Bela Lugosi (1882–1956) so loved playing Dracula that in one interview Lugosi said to a reporter, "Dracula will never end." So it would only be fitting that he be buried with the black cape he once swirled around his body before he was about to bite his victims. Thankfully, Hollywood's dark prince has not been reported to leave his grave like the film's character does.

JOHN WILKES BOOTH

May 10, 1838–April 26, 1865

SAVING HIS NECK

John Wilkes Booth had a flare for the dramatic. In fact, if he had not assassinated President Abraham Lincoln, then Booth would have been remembered as one of the greatest theater actors of his day, not to mention a real heartthrob. One newspaper called him "the most handsome man on the American stage." The dark-haired, debonair actor was such a stud that he received more than a hundred love letters a week and an income of twenty thousand dollars yearly (a millionaire by today's standards). Booth's killing Lincoln would be kind of like a Hollywood A-lister shooting the president today.* Mix in a possible government cover-up, and you have all the makings of a true Hollywood drama.

On April 14, 1865, Lincoln was attending a play at Ford's Theatre, when Booth stepped inside the presidential box and fired a derringer pistol at the back of the president's head. Lincoln slumped forward. Booth jumped from the balcony, breaking his leg as he fell. He made his way across the stage and out a darkened side door, causing many in the audience to believe his appearance was part of the play.

A twelve-day manhunt for Booth ensued, ending in a standoff in the

---

*Ryan Gosling also happens to bear an uncanny resemblance to Booth.

early morning hours of April 26. Twenty-six Union soldiers surrounded Booth and his accomplice, David Herold, in an old tobacco barn in Port Royal, Virginia. The officers had strict orders—take Booth out alive.

That wasn't an easy task, considering Booth swore he would never be captured. He was already a complete mess—crippled and more than just a little annoyed that the rest of the country wasn't thanking him for shooting Lincoln. The actor-turned-murderer just wasn't giving up without a fight. The officers considered their options. Once the sun rose, they would become easy target practice for Booth, who just happened to be an excellent shot.* They had to get him out of that barn before sunrise. If a blaze of glory was what Booth wanted, a blaze of glory was what he would get. They would smoke him out.

The officers gathered pine twigs and placed them at the side of the barn. They lit the kindling, and within seconds the barn's dry, weathered boards were set aglow. Booth looked to the door as the light of the flames danced in his widened eyes. The crack of a pistol rang out. Booth fell face forward. At first no one knew who fired the shot. A man named Sergeant Corbett would later claim that he shot Booth because "Providence" had directed him.**

---

*He killed Lincoln with one shot, but we won't count that since he was so close to Lincoln's head.
**Insanity also directed him. Corbett had once cut out a very important part of his anatomy in his nether regions to avoid temptation from the ladies. I hear this does the trick.

The soldiers quickly moved into the barn and dragged the dying man out. They placed him on a mattress away from the flames and examined his wound. The shot had gone through his neck, paralyzing his body. Booth opened his eyes and tried to move his lips. He hung on for about three hours, and then, just as the sun was coming up over the horizon, he uttered his last words: "useless, useless."

Booth's possessions were then seized, including five pictures of girlfriends (he probably had more), a compass, an appointment book that he had used as his diary, and a stickpin engraved with his name. The soldiers identified Booth by the initials *JWB*, which were tattooed on his hand.

Strangely, there were some details of that night that left soldiers confused. Booth was not wearing the signet ring and watch he always wore. Two of the soldiers noticed that the man pulled from the barn had red hair and freckles. Booth had jet-black hair and didn't have any freckles. Booth was also dressed in a Confederate uniform. Several witnesses, including Dr. Mudd, who had set Booth's broken leg days earlier, had reported that he was wearing a black suit.

Then there was the leg injury. Dr. Mudd had reported that Booth's injury was "a straight fracture of the tibia about two inches above the ankle" on his left leg. Dr. May, the doctor who examined Booth after his death, reported that Booth's "right limb was greatly contused and perfectly black from a fracture of one of the long bones." One doctor claimed the injury was on the left. The other claimed the right. Was it possible that Union soldiers had killed someone other than Booth, or was their recollection of the night simply clouded by all the drama?

The body was then taken by steamship to the official autopsy in Washington. During the examinations, doctors removed Booth's vertebrae from where the bullet had passed, and carefully wrapped them in brown paper to be cataloged by the Army Medical Museum. Booth's body was then buried under the floor of the Washington, DC, Arsenal Penitentiary. In 1869, at the request of Booth's family, the body was moved to an unmarked grave in Baltimore, Maryland.

Flash forward more than one hundred years later, and those simple neck bones would become the key to unlocking the mystery of who really died at that barn on April 26, 1865. In 2010 Booth's relatives and historians made plans to exhume the body of Booth's brother, Edwin, to test the vertebrae's DNA against Edwin's DNA. If the DNA matched, then the case would be closed—John Wilkes Booth died in the barn. If it didn't match . . . well, some people had some history books to rewrite. It seemed like a simple way to solve the mystery. Unfortunately, the Armed Forces Institute for Pathology didn't see it that way. They worried that taking even a small sample of DNA might destroy a piece of history. They denied the request for a DNA sample.

Many Booth historians today believe that the *JWB* on Booth's hand was not John Wilkes Booth's initials, but James William Boyd's initials. Boyd was a confederate spy hired by

Secretary of War Edwin M. Stanton. Rumors circulated during this time that Stanton was involved in a plot to kidnap President Lincoln. It was well known that he didn't care for Honest Abe, referring to him as a long-legged ape who suffered from "painful imbecility."* But did he hate Lincoln enough to plot his death? Stanton did possess the one documented glimpse into Booth's motives—his diary. This diary disappeared shortly after Booth's death. Two years later it turned up again. Curiously, eighteen pages of the diary were torn out. Could the diary have incriminated Stanton?

Many questions remain unanswered. One thing is certain. John Wilkes Booth would probably have loved all the ballyhoo. America's most famous assassin may someday stick his neck out from the grave and stir up even more drama.

Where are they now?

John Wilkes Booth's neck bones are stored in the National Museum of Health and Medicine in Silver Spring, MD. Also in the museum's collection are skull fragments, locks of hair, and the bloodied suit cuffs of Abraham Lincoln. Booth's missing diary pages have never been found.

---

*He did have long legs. Lincoln was six feet four. Most historians would disagree with the imbecile part.

ANOTHER SPINY TALE

KING RICHARD III *(1452–1485)*

If the body of King Richard III could talk, it would have a whole lot of complaints. It might say something like, "How dare that Shakespeare call me a hunchback!" Or "Okay, people, where are my clothes, and hello . . . where are my feet?" And lastly, "Is this parking lot a fitting burial place for the bones of a king of England?" The last complaint would have most historians answering with a resounding *no*.

In 1485 Richard III died at the battle of Bosworth Field while he was fighting forces that were led by the head of the Tudor family, Henry VII. After Richard was killed, Henry VII crowned himself king, and then he and subsequent Tudors went on a massive smear campaign to discredit Richard. A century later, while on the Tudor payroll, William Shakespeare became the biggest trash talker. He wrote plays about Richard where he called him a "lump of foul deformity" and portrayed Richard as a power-hungry hunchback who drowned his brother in a casket of malmsey wine (false), poisoned his wife (false), and murdered his two nephews to clear his path to the throne (we may never know).*

---

*Richard III's nephews, Edward and Richard, are another case of lost bodies. Historians suspect that they are buried either in the Tower of London or in Saint George's Chapel in Windsor Castle.

After his defeat, Richard's body was stripped of its clothing and displayed as a trophy. Legend had it that his corpse was either thrown into a river or buried at a nearby church. Desperate to solve the over five-hundred-year-old mystery, in September 2012 historians began searching for King Richard's body under a parking lot in Leicester that had once been the site of Greyfriars Church. They immediately found a body stuffed into a too-small grave and missing its feet. The skeleton had nine wounds inflicted on the head and two to the body. DNA matched to the last two surviving Richard III descendants showed that researchers had finally found King Richard III's body.

His skeletal remains revealed several clues. Richard had died in his thirties, had had a slender build, and had suffered from scoliosis—a curvature of the spine that would have caused one shoulder to be higher than the other. (The skeleton did not show a hunchback, like Shakespeare claimed.) Other interesting clues revealed that Richard had the intestinal parasite roundworm, had severe arthritis, drank at least a bottle of wine a day, and like most high-born men, ate mostly meat. Scientists were even able to use his skull to reconstruct his face, and it turns out Richard wasn't that shabby-looking.*

On March 26, 2015, Richard III's remains were finally given a more regal view than his earlier parking lot grave. He is now buried in Leicester Cathedral in Leicester, UK.

---

*I will let you be the judge. Just google "Richard III's facial reconstruction."

SARAH BERNHARDT

October 22, 1844–March 26, 1923

The
DIVINE
SARAH

BREAK A LEG

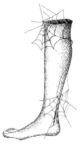

You just never know what you are going to find when you tidy up. It began as a simple task of dusting the cobwebs off skulls and jarred fetuses. That was when the staff of Bordeaux University's medical school in Paris stumbled upon something odd . . . an amputated leg. But it wasn't just any leg. It was the leg of Sarah Bernhardt, the most famous actress of the nineteenth century. In a statement to the press, the Bordeaux University insisted, "We never actually lost the leg. It was just forgotten."* How Sarah Bernhardt's leg was "forgotten" in a medical school's storage room is a bit of a mystery.

Let's start with the leg's owner. Sarah Bernhardt's life was dramatic well before she lost her leg. She watched her son be mauled by ferocious tigers. She murdered her lovers with hat pins and hatchets. She was stabbed, poisoned, strangled, and burned to death. And then . . . the curtain fell.

That was her life onstage. But her real life was just as theatrical. She was born in Breton outside of Paris in October 1844. It is unknown who her father was, but her mother was a Jewish girl from Amsterdam. As a child, Sarah was the kind of kid who got her way by throwing her

---

*It is really easy to forget you once had a leg when your skull collection gets out of control.

small body around in spasmodic tantrums. When that didn't work, she reverted to her usual flair for the dramatic. Once, when her mom insisted she eat her panade—a gruel made from bread and butter—Sarah swallowed black ink instead. She immediately became violently ill and screamed at her mother, "It is you who have killed me!" Her mother fainted. Sarah was never asked to eat panade again.

When Sarah was nine years old, her mother decided to move her into a convent to straighten her up. One problem—Sarah didn't want to go. So she threw more tantrums, used foul language that we won't repeat, slapped the nuns when they tried to brush her hair, and tried to run away. Over time, she grew to love the convent (although she still threw her tantrums). She was given a small plot for a garden where she collected animals—crickets, lizards, and spiders. When her mother returned for Sarah, she said to the mother superior, "You have mastered my little wild animal." "Oh no!" cried the clever mother superior. "I have merely tamed her." Anyone who tried to cage Sarah's spirit didn't get very far.

When Sarah was fifteen, her mother decided it was time for her daughter to marry. Sarah would have none of it. Marriage meant someone could boss you around. Instead she tossed her frizzy golden hair in the air, looked to the heavens, and with her flutelike voice proclaimed, "I will be a nun. I will!" It was a performance worthy of an Oscar. At least her mother thought so. The next day Sarah began acting lessons at the Conservatoire acting school.*

It turns out that this was the right decision. Sarah Bernhardt went on to become the most beloved actress of her day. Death scenes were her specialty. Sometimes she faked death so well that people thought she had really died. Sarah had a morbid fascination with death. One of her favorite pastimes was to visit the Paris morgue to see the unclaimed bodies on display. She owned a skull that she used as a letter holder and a pet skeleton named Lazarus.** Strangest of all, she slept in a rosewood coffin lined with white satin. It looked comfy, but really freaked out her friends.

The public couldn't get enough of the Divine Sarah and her coffin-sleeping shenanigans. The press followed Sarah's every move, gleefully reporting on her antics. And there were a lot of antics. Sarah traveled

*This may sound like every girl's dream, but acting was not the respected craft that it is today. Most actresses were viewed as lower-class women who would never be invited for tea and crumpets at any respectable lady's home.
**Lazarus was named for the Christian biblical story of the man who rose from the dead. Obviously, Sarah's skeleton wasn't coming back to life anytime soon.

with her own private zoo—at least three dogs, a parrot, a monkey, a cheetah, a few lion cubs, seven chameleons, a boa constrictor, and an alligator named Ali-Gaga.* She was always covered in furs, scarves, veils, and jingling bells. Sometimes she wore a hat with a stuffed bat on it—a hard look to pull off, but not for Sarah.

Her Paris fans (whom she called her "beloved monsters") adored Sarah so much they held a Sarah Bernhardt Day. Emperors and princes showered her with gifts. Queens were brought to tears by her performances. The novelist Victor Hugo was so enchanted with Sarah he sent her a letter that

---

*Some of her animals didn't fare so well. Ali-Gaga ate one of the dogs, and the boa constrictor had to be shot when it ate the sofa pillows.

read, *The tear which you drew from me belongs to you. I place it at your feet.* He enclosed with his letter a tear-shaped diamond. Poet Oscar Wilde threw lilies at her feet and called her "the greatest tragic actress of any stage."

When Sarah toured in America, fans rushed at her, begging for "autographs"—the new American custom of having a star sign her name on a piece of paper. When one adoring fan couldn't find ink, she cut her arm and used her own blood. Thomas Edison, the most famous inventor of his day (p. 160), was utterly smitten with Sarah. She visited him in his home in New Jersey, and he let her try out one of his new inventions—a recording device called a phonograph. In America, Sarah gave one hundred and fifty performances in fifty-one cities. This grueling schedule would have exhausted most stars, but not Sarah. She had her way of getting occasional breaks from the press. Sometimes to avoid giving interviews, she would pretend to faint. Then, once the annoying reporter was gone, she would skip around the room.

Her skipping days ended after a fall during the play *La Tosca*. She was supposed to fling herself from atop a castle wall in a mock suicide. Unfortunately, the mattress that was used to break her fall had been moved, and Sarah landed on the cold, hard floor, injuring her right kneecap. Over the years, Sarah's leg got worse and worse until amputation was the only option. Did Sarah throw one of her infamous tantrums? *Mais non.* She didn't throw tantrums over things she couldn't change. In fact, she greeted the removal of her leg with the enthusiasm of a debutante attending her first ball. In one letter she gushed, "So happy my leg is cut off tomorrow."

After the surgery on February 22, 1915, the leg was immediately sent over to the Bordeaux medical facility, where the knee was dissected. The diagnosis was "joint tuberculosis," which is a fancy way of saying Sarah's leg had become a fetid mass of decaying flesh. Legend has it that circus showman P. T. Barnum offered Sarah ten thousand dollars for her amputated leg, to which Sarah replied, "If it's my right leg you want, see the doctors; if it's the left leg, see my manager in New York."* Instead the leg sat in storage. Why it was saved is anyone's guess. Perhaps autographs were not enough to remember the Divine Sarah.

Sarah was given a wooden leg and some crutches, but she preferred to be carried around in a covered divan chair like a Byzantine princess. She continued to work, taking shorter roles and ones that didn't require her to

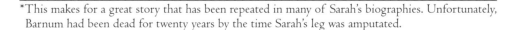

*This makes for a great story that has been repeated in many of Sarah's biographies. Unfortunately, Barnum had been dead for twenty years by the time Sarah's leg was amputated.

throw herself from high places. When Sarah was seventy-eight years old, her kidneys started to give out, and she took to her bed. Fans crowded outside her Paris apartment, waiting for news. Always tragic to the end, Sarah wouldn't give them the satisfaction of dying quickly and quipped, "I will keep them hanging." And so she did and always will.

Where are they now?

The leg still resides in Bordeaux University's medical school in France. Many historians have doubts about whether it is really Sarah's leg, due to its missing label. DNA testing has yet to be performed to clear up any uncertainties.

YOU'RE PULLING MY LEG

Before the discovery of antibiotics, wounds could be extremely dangerous if they became infected. Consequently, battlefield surgeons were often forced to amputate soldiers' limbs to save their lives.

ALL HAIL THE LEG

Sometimes only a person's body parts become famous and not the whole person. Most people don't know who Henry Paget, second Earl of Uxbridge, was, but his leg has certainly caused its

share of ruckus. In 1815 Uxbridge commanded a cavalry in the battle of Waterloo, where his right leg was injured by a cannonball. After the battle, Uxbridge was moved to Monsieur Paris's house, where surgeons were forced to amputate his leg. Paris, clearly crushing on Uxbridge's bravery, asked to save the leg and bury it in his garden. He then built a shrine to the leg, even giving it its own tombstone. People from all over Europe came to see Uxbridge's leg, and Paris made a small fortune from curious tourists.*
Then one day one of these tourists happened to be Uxbridge's son. By this point, the leg bone was being displayed openly, and Uxbridge Junior was none too happy to see Pop's leg on the wall. His son demanded the leg be returned, but Paris refused. The fight for the leg became a whole melee, with the Belgium ambassador demanding the leg be returned to the family. The leg was hidden away until Paris's death in 1934, when

---

*Like I keep saying . . . there is profit to be made from body parts.

his widow found it in the study. Probably tired of the bickering and realizing that it just simply didn't match the drapes . . . she incinerated it in her central-heating furnace.

GETTING A FOOT IN THE DOOR

Impressing your lady friends is not always easy. You need charm, good looks, and smarts, and a severed limb never hurts. Such was the case for Civil War general Daniel Edgar Sickles. In 1863, in Gettysburg, Pennsylvania, Sickles's leg was crushed by a cannonball and amputated. Most legs were just left in piles outside the field hospital, but Sickles was rather fond of his leg. He kept his leg in a coffin-shaped box. Years later he mailed it to the Army Medical Museum in Washington, DC, as a keepsake.* Sickles was then rumored to take his lady friends to the museum to show off his lost limb.** You can still find Sickles's leg at the National Museum of Health and Medicine in Washington, DC.

---

*It may seem uncouth to mail a leg to someone, but Sickles did include his calling card.
**This will work only on some girls.

VINCENT VAN GOGH

March 30, 1853–July 29, 1890

LEND ME YOUR EAR

We have all experienced it. Someone gives you a present that wasn't exactly what you had in mind. You try to be polite, but the disappointment is hard to hide. On December 23, 1888, a young woman named Rachel experienced such a moment.

Her friend Vincent van Gogh staggered into her home and handed her a small package wrapped in newspaper. His gift came with stern instructions: "Guard this object very carefully." Since it was a couple of days before Christmas, Rachel may have been expecting a special gift . . . like jewels. Or perhaps a pretty hair comb? But knowing Vincent's eccentric ways, she may have also braced herself for something more unusual.

To start, Vincent had some bad habits. He was fond of a green drink called absinthe, which made him act like he had punched too many holes in his crazy card. He also liked to eat yellow paint after it had fallen onto the floor and mixed with dirt.* If only he had chosen blue or green, he might have been only half-bonkered, but yellow paint contained poisonous lead. When ingested, lead causes all sorts of nuttiness.

No one in the small town of Arles, France, had much respect for

---

*It must have given it some flavor.

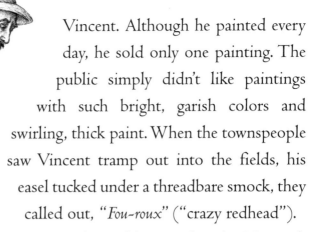

Vincent. Although he painted every day, he sold only one painting. The public simply didn't like paintings with such bright, garish colors and swirling, thick paint. When the townspeople saw Vincent tramp out into the fields, his easel tucked under a threadbare smock, they called out, *"Fou-roux"* ("crazy redhead").

On that cold December day, Vincent's flaming red hair was tucked under a beret slanted to the left, and he was acting even more erratic than usual. Rachel peeled back the thin layers of newspaper and saw the tiny words from yesterday's news stained red. Blood red. Inside, a flesh-colored mound emerged from its cocoon. When Rachel realized it was an ear, she did what any sensible person would do to avoid that awkward gift-giving moment. She fainted.

Today van Gogh is often remembered as much for what he did with his razor blade as what he did with his paintbrush. The ear incident has left many historians wondering just how messed up in the head was Vincent van Gogh. Was he really crazy enough to lop off his own ear?

Historians have come up with every illness in the book to explain his actions—epilepsy, manic depression, bipolar disorder,

Mmmm . . . paint.
Delicious!

porphyria, sunstroke, and syphilis, to name a few. Perhaps van Gogh's steady diet of absinthe and lead paint made him daffy enough to reach for a blade? Maybe. But psychologists have long insisted that self-mutilators tend to go for arms and fingers. Ears are never on the hit list. Cutting off your ear tends to get pretty messy too, but van Gogh's ear was sliced off as clean as a stick of butter.

So if Vincent didn't cut off his ear, who did? Many historians have pointed the finger at his pal Paul Gauguin, who at the time was rooming with him. Up to this point, the two had been fighting constantly, and both were easily angered. Van Gogh even threw a glass of absinthe at Gauguin's head. Fortunately, it missed, but Gauguin got the message— his friend was coming undone.

That left Gauguin with a motive: he was utterly sick of van Gogh. He also had the means: a fierce temper and a fencing sword that he kept on him at all times. But probably the most convincing evidence was the forensics. The ear was cut off so perfectly that doctors immediately

The ear is not the only relic lost to history. After Vincent's death, his mother threw many of his paintings in the trash. (She was never a fan.)

asked van Gogh who had cut him. Cutting off your own ear is hard enough. Doing it in one fell swoop is next to impossible.

But here is where the case grows cold—the witness testimony. The strongest witness was the victim, later found bleeding in his bed beneath his bright yellow sunflower paintings. He wasn't talking. When doctors asked van Gogh how he happened to be missing his ear, he merely replied that is was "quite personal."*

Gauguin didn't stick around to be questioned either. The day after the ear-cutting incident, he packed up his bags quicker than you can say "manic" and headed back to Paris. Vincent later wrote cryptic letters to Gauguin, even saying at one point, "I will keep quiet about this and so will you." Gauguin never wrote back, but in a letter to another friend he said of his old roommate, "A man with sealed lips, I cannot complain about him."

On July 27, 1890, van Gogh set out for the wheat fields he always loved with his easel tucked under his arm. He returned by nightfall, clutching his stomach. Van Gogh had shot himself. When questioned

---

*The need for privacy is strange when you consider that a missing ear is a bit hard to keep private. People are bound to ask all sorts of questions like, "Say, Vinny, where did your ear go? I could have sworn you had one yesterday."

by authorities as to why he committed suicide, van Gogh replied, "My body is mine and I am free to do what I want with it."

On a positive note, art critics found a new appreciation for van Gogh's art after he put that bullet in his stomach.* In 1987 one of van Gogh's sunflower paintings sold for 8.1 million dollars. The following year, his painting *Irises* sold for 53.9 million. Not bad for a crazy redhead.

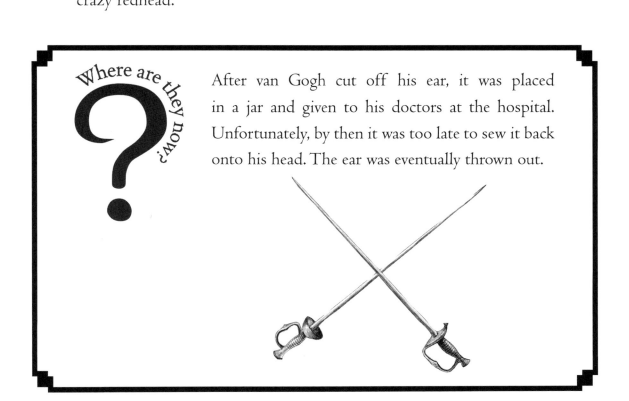

Where are they now?

After van Gogh cut off his ear, it was placed in a jar and given to his doctors at the hospital. Unfortunately, by then it was too late to sew it back onto his head. The ear was eventually thrown out.

---

*People are funny like that.

ARTSY EXTRAS

THE *MONA LISA* *(1479–1542)*

Some of the best secrets really do go to the grave. One such secret is the identity of the woman in the *Mona Lisa*, painted by Leonardo da Vinci (1452–1519). It has long been suspected that the woman with the famed

smile is Lisa Gherardini, the wife of an Italian silk merchant. In 2015 scientists compared the DNA from skeletons known to be those of her children to the DNA of a skeleton suspected to be Lisa. Unfortunately, the DNA from her children's skeletons was too deteriorated to make a match with 100 percent certainty. If scientists can ever find a close enough match, they can then use the skeleton's bone structure to make a virtual reconstruction of her face and know once and for all what the Mona Lisa really looked like.

WOLFGANG AMADEUS MOZART *(1756–1791)*

In eighteenth-century Vienna, getting your own grave was like getting a mansion to romp around in. Very few people were given such a luxury. In most cases, bodies were piled on top of one another in the same hole,

Grandma?

Um . . . no.

or even worse . . . cleared to make room for new bodies. This led to a lot of confusion when people tried to find remains. Fortunately for the great composer Mozart, the sexton who watched over his grave was a big fan. He made a note of where Mozart was buried by twisting a piece of wire around Mozart's neck. When the graveyard was cleared in 1801, he rushed in to save Mozart's skull. The skull was then passed down through family members. In 2006 scientists ran DNA tests to compare the skull's DNA with Mozart's grandmother and his niece buried nearby. Not only did the skulls' DNA not match Mozart's DNA, but the grandmother and niece also did not match each other. This means that Mozart's relatives have some explaining to do.*

FRANCISCO GOYA *(1746–1828)*

Skeletons and skulls are sort of like socks. It's so annoying when they don't match. At least the Spanish council should have thought so when they opened the coffin of painter Francisco Goya. Goya had died in Bordeaux, France, in 1828, estranged from his Spanish homeland. In 1901 the Spanish government got permission to rebury him on Spanish soil, but when they opened his coffin . . .

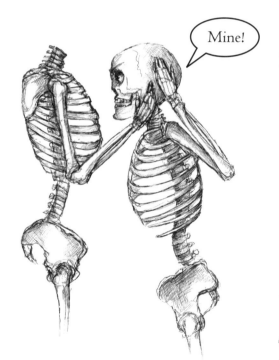

Mine!

they found two skeletons and only one skull. On further examination, authorities concluded that the skull most likely

---

*What that explanation entails is beyond the scope of this book.

belonged to the other skeleton, whose identity remains a mystery. Even more puzzling was what happened to Goya's skull. No one ever bothered to sort out the mess. Instead they just buried Goya's headless skeleton with his companion at the Chapel of St. Anthony of Florida in Madrid. To this day the location of Goya's skull remains a mystery.

CREEPY PORTRAITS

Everyone knows that it is easier to paint a portrait from a live model than from memory. So what do you do when you don't have a live model?

You use a dead one! That is what had to be done for the portrait of James Scott, the Duke of Monmouth. James was executed for treason in 1685. The court wanted a family portrait of James but . . . oops, they had already chopped off his head. The solution: they dug up James's body and had a surgeon sew his head back on.

DEATH'S MONA LISA

She is known as l'Inconnue de la Seine, and you might have kissed her. Around the late 1880s, a girl's body was fished from the Seine River and taken to the Paris morgue. Believed to be a suicide, she had no markings on her body, and her identity was never known. But what was remarkable was the peaceful smile on her face and her perfect features. She looked like an angel sleeping. The pathologist at the morgue was so taken

with her beauty that he made a death mask—a plaster casting of her face. The resulting casting was so exquisite that it was widely reproduced by artists and hung in Parisian homes as a trendy, albeit morbid, wall decoration. So why have you probably kissed her? L'Inconnue de la Seine's face also became the model for CPR Annie or Resusci Anne—the most popular CPR doll on the market today.

A PICTURE SAYS TOO MANY WORDS

If kissing a dead French girl didn't creep you out . . . then this one surely will. But first let's get serious for a moment and think about one depressing fact: before the invention of photography, most people had no way to remember the image of a loved one. They died, and all the living had were memories and a few strands of hair. The invention of the first commercially produced photographs, called daguerreotypes, in 1839 changed all of that. Only one problem. Daguerreotypes were expensive. Very expensive. So the only photograph most families could ever afford to take of a loved one was the one after they died. This last photograph was called a mourning portrait. In the photo shoot, the deceased were propped up with their cheeks tinted pink and their eyelids pinned open. Sometimes they were even posed next to surviving loved ones. The photographs were then made into postcards and sent to grieving family members.*

---

*This is the only time I am going to ask you not to google.

MERCY BROWN

1873–January 17, 1892

A HEARTLESS VAMPIRE

In 1892 death was contagious. You could catch it from your brother, your sister, your mother, or even your neighbor. The signs of death approaching were always the same: First the afflicted became pale and thin. Then came a hacking, bloody cough. Over time the person got weaker and weaker. At this point death was called "consumption" or the "wasting sickness," because it literally did just that—slowly wasted away your body. We know it today as tuberculosis, but people back then did not call it that. They didn't even realize tuberculosis was contagious.

It was especially prevalent in the rural town of Exeter, Rhode Island, where the population had dipped from 2,500 in 1820 to only 961 by 1862.* But instead of believing diseases were contagious, New Englanders believed death was contagious. In that small, desolate town, dead people infected the living. It all made perfect sense. The undead would creep out of their graves at night and feed on the blood of unsuspecting family members, leaving them pale and lifeless.

Wait a minute, you say . . . does this sound a lot like a vampire?

---

*American Civil War casualties (1861–1865) were also responsible for the population dip. Of course, a large percentage of people who died during the Civil War died from diseases such as tuberculosis.

The real reason why Mercy's body had not decomposed as much as her mother's and siblings' bodies was because it was kept in a crypt during the winter months, thereby slowing down the decomposition rate.

But New Englanders didn't call these bloodsuckers "vampires." That sounded way too hocus-pocus. Plus, they were far too rational for that kind of nonsense.* They just knew that some supernatural force was at work. They didn't dare name it.

Such was the case with the Brown family. On December 8, 1883, thirty-six-year-old Mary Eliza Brown died of consumption, leaving behind a husband and six children. Six months later her daughter Mary

---

*Rhode Islanders also did not believe in witches. You could not be tried as a witch in Rhode Island. You had to go to Massachusetts for that, because that was where all the crazies lived.

Olive followed her to the grave. A few years later the son, Edwin, also fell ill and moved to Colorado Springs, where he believed the fresh air might improve his health. While he was gone, his nineteen-year-old sister, Mercy (called Lena), also fell ill and died from the same disease. When Edwin returned, his health began to decline rapidly. The townsfolk were terrified—death was going around the Brown family. Like most people of the time, they believed that someone from the recently deceased Brown family was feeding on Edwin's warm blood. They certainly didn't want such a demon moving on to the next helpless family. Something had to be done. Something horrible.

So with much pressure from the town, the father, George Brown, agreed to have the bodies of the three women dug up. It may sound strange, but this had been done before in many other New England towns. You see, there was a simple procedure supported by medical professionals of the time to tell if someone was not really, truly, 100 percent, without a doubt dead. First off, the body had to be decomposed to the right level of nastiness or the deceased would be suspect (see p. viii). Second, the heart must not have any blood left in it. If both checked out . . . sure enough, the person was good and dead.

When the townsfolk pried opened the coffin of the mother, Mary Eliza, the medical examiner breathed a sigh of relief. The body was in the proper state of putrefaction with "nothing exceptional existing." Then they peeked in on the daughter Mary Olive, and she was just a mess—a decomposed skeleton overgrown with hair.* Lastly, the medical examiner lifted the top of Mercy's wood coffin and found something

---

*Despite the well-known myth, hair and nails do not keep growing after you are dead, but corpses do tend to look more hairy. The reason for the hairiness is because after death the body dehydrates, causing the skin to pull back toward the skull, thereby making it appear like there is more hair.

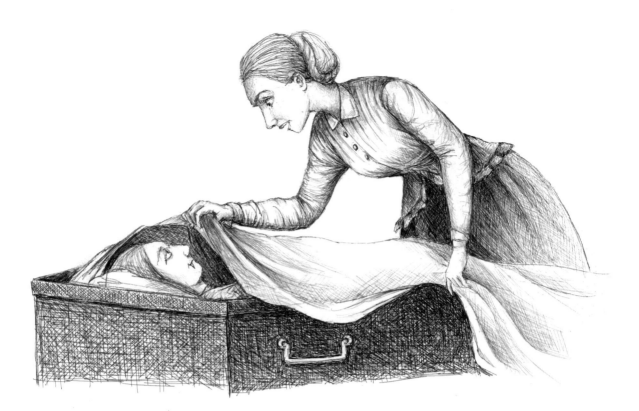

entirely different. Her cheeks still had color, and she had not rotted the same amount as the rest of the family. Then the medical examiner cut open her heart and found it still dripping with blood. The culprit was found. Mercy Brown was feeding on her brother.

You might want to put down your lunch for the next part of this story. An old Native American cure had been passed down to the people of New England. According to this cure, the only way to save Edwin was to drink a special sort of chicken soup. Except this soup didn't have chicken. No, the soup Edwin drank contained the burned heart of his sister Mercy. Yum.

Edwin drank the diabolical concoction. He died two months later and was left to rest in peace. His sister was not so lucky. The story of her undead heart haunts the people of Exeter, Rhode Island. Every year curious tourists visit her cemetery and place strange things on her grave—knives, cough drops, roses, and the occasional set of vampire teeth. Legend has it that she haunts an old bridge near where she is buried, appearing in a tattered white dress and smelling of roses. If Mercy Brown is haunting Exeter, Rhode Island, you can bet she is now truly, without a doubt, dead.

Where are they now?

You can visit Mercy Brown at the cemetery behind the Chestnut Hill Baptist Church in Exeter, Rhode Island. Next to her gravestone, you can still find the rock that Mercy's heart was burned on. Many people have noted that very little grass grows on her grave. It would be fun to speculate that this is because

Mercy's undead spirit roams the cemetery, ripping up the grass. In reality, it is because too many people have walked across her grave and killed the grass. If you visit her grave, bring a cross and some garlic. Please stay off the lawn.

THE DEAD VS. THE UNDEAD (A FIELD GUIDE)

It takes a certain amount of expertise to know the difference between the dead and the undead. You should use the following clues to identify a vampire.

SIZE

A vampire will look a bit plumper after a night of indulging in too much blood.* A body will also look bloated due to the bacteria in the body feeding on the decomposing stomach instead of food in the digestive track. This process produces gas . . . lots of gas. When we are alive and moving around, this gas gets expelled.** When we are dead this gas builds up in the stomach with nowhere to go, causing belly bloat.***

---

*Never tell a female vampire that she looks "plump." First, it is just rude. Second, it is entirely unfair since vampires cannot look in mirrors.

**How it gets expelled is beyond the scope of this book.

***Actually, eventually it does get expelled when the small intestine collapses. You really don't want to be around a dead person when this happens.

STAKING

A staked vampire will naturally scream after being staked, because driving a piece of wood through your heart sort of hurts. The dead will also scream due to natural gases escaping from the chest cavity. This scream sounds more like a balloon losing air quickly and less like an I-am-so-ticked-off-that-you-just-drove-a-stake-through-my-heart sort of scream.

BLOOD AROUND LIPS

Vampires are not the most polite creatures and will sometimes forget to wipe their mouths with

their napkins after a meal. Around their mouths the dead will also have dark-red decomposition fluid called purge fluid, which can resemble blood.

PALENESS

You won't see a vampire with a golden glow. The dead also look pale, but for different reasons. When a body decomposes, gravity forces the blood downward. Less blood in your face means less of a rosy glow.

MATA HARI

August 7, 1876–October 15, 1917

I SPY A HEAD

If only there were a lost-and-found location for body parts, the world would be a better place. Of course, one would think if you went through the trouble to save someone's head, you might have the common decency to put it in a safe place.* Such was not the case when the Museum of Anatomy in Paris lost the head of Mata Hari, one of the most notorious spies in history.

It's kind of easy to see why the head was lost when you consider to whom it belonged. People either adored Mata Hari or hated her guts. They called her a liar, a thief, a hussy, a spendthrift, a spy, and a bunch of other things we won't repeat. They also called her fascinating, artistic, beautiful, exotic, and "one of the most charming specimens of female humanity." To this day, no one can even agree on whether she was a spy. But one thing is certain: if Mata Hari was a spy, she was rather bad at it.

What she was good at was lying. Even her name was a lie. She was born Margaretha Geertruida Zelle in the small Dutch town of Leeuwarden. Her father owned a successful hat shop that allowed him to spoil little "Margreet" with exclusive schools, fine clothing, and even

---

*People are funny like that.

her own miniature carriage pulled by two white goats. Margreet didn't look much like the other Dutch kids. Most Dutch kids had fair skin and blond hair, and they were buttoned up to the chin in staid black dresses. Margreet had dark skin, ebony-colored hair, and wore red-and-yellow-striped dresses like some cancan girl. Of course, red-and-yellow dresses were all the rage in her "castle" (lie) that she inherited from her noble ancestors (bigger lie). It was the start of a dramatic life.

Unfortunately, tragedy struck when Margreet was just thirteen years old. Her father went bankrupt and ran off with another woman. Shortly after, her mother died, leaving Margreet to stay with relatives. Without money or social standing, Margreet's marriage prospects were slim. It didn't help that she was five feet seven and flat-chested in an age when a curvy figure was the ideal.* Still, Margreet was extremely pretty and did not have any problem getting dates.

In 1895 she married Dutch Colonial Army Captain Rudolf MacLeod and shortly after moved to the exotic island of Java in the Dutch East Indies (today Indonesia). In Java, Margreet soaked up the culture—the brightly colored clothing, the lush vegetation, and especially the local dances. She would later incorporate these dances into her own style of dance.

Margreet's stay in Java was not a happy one. Her husband was a big jerk. He beat her with a cat-o'-nine-tails (a nine-pronged whip), drank too much, and didn't give her any money for fancy hats. In 1903 Margreet filed for legal separation and ran away to Paris because she thought "all women who ran away from their husbands went to Paris." It turns out Margreet was anything but "all women."

---

*Typically, heights in the nineteenth century were much shorter. A British male officer averaged no more than five feet, five inches. Mata Hari would be the equivalent of six feet tall today.

While in Paris, she became an exotic dancer and, to sound more glamorous, changed her name to Mata Hari, meaning "the eye of the day" in Javanese. Margreet called her veiled dancing "temple dances" and "sacred poems." Today we would just call it belly dancing with a lot of sparkly things, but no one back then had ever seen such a thing. As the newly reinvented Mata Hari, the truth was cast away as easily as her veils. According to Mata Hari, she was born in India to a Brahman family (lie) and her mother was a temple dancer (bigger lie). The public ate it up, and Mata Hari made a fortune.

Then in 1914, World War I broke out while Mata Hari was in Berlin. The war put France and Britain on one side and Germany on another. Suddenly no one cared to see an aging, exotic dancer wave veils around. People were now more interested in things like avoiding bombs falling from the sky. That was when Mata Hari decided to move back to Holland and reinvent herself yet again—as a German spy.

While in Holland, the German consul gave her invisible ink, twenty thousand francs, and the code name H21. They may have even sent her to spy school. All and all, it could have been the start of an illustrious career if it had not been for one problem: Mata Hari really stank at being a spy. She was probably the worst spy in the history of spying. Part of her problem was follow-through. She took the money but tossed the invisible ink in the ocean. Some biographers claim she never had any intention of spying for Germany. Either way, French and British counterintelligence got word that she was a spy and were determined to bring her down. By the time Mata Hari was back in Paris, she was being constantly tailed, her letters were steamed open, and her suitcases were repeatedly ransacked when she left her hotel.

And here is where the story gets confusing. French Intelligence believed the quickest way to get evidence on her was to ask her to become a French spy—sort of like calling her bluff with a double bluff. Mata Hari needed the money, so she agreed. Unfortunately, she was not much better at being a French spy than she was at being a German one. She did pass on a few bits of information, but nothing of any great value. Whether trivial or not, she sent the information via regular mail and did not bother to use code or invisible ink. That was when the Germans most likely figured out that Mata Hari was spying for the French. To expose her to their enemies, the Germans then sent secret telegrams in a code that they knew the French had already cracked years prior. The French intercepted and read the letters. The contents identified Mata Hari as the German spy H21. The French now had their evidence.

On February 13, 1917, Mata Hari was arrested by French authorities and sent to Saint-Lazare prison. Her trial was a complete sham. Other than the telegrams, no concrete evidence could be found showing that she had ever passed French military secrets on to the Germans. Mata Hari did admit to taking money from the Germans, but she denied ever doing any work for them. It turns out . . . pretending to be a spy can get you in as much trouble as actually being a spy.

On October 15, 1917, at the age of forty-one, Mata Hari was lined up in front of a firing squad of twelve French officers. She reportedly went to her death bravely, refusing the blindfold, and blowing the priest a kiss before shots rang out across the misty field. As was customary at the time for criminals, her body was sent to the Museum of Anatomy in Paris, where her head was severed and preserved in wax. Rumor has it that one of her many admirers stole the head. Others believe the head was lost when the museum was moved in 1954. Much like the enigmatic dancer, the truth may never be revealed.

Where are they now?

Although the Museum of Anatomy in Paris is still missing Mata Hari's head, it does contain hundreds of skeletons, miscellaneous teeth, jarred fetuses, and diseased body parts— good, old-fashioned fun for the whole family.

LOST AND NEVER FOUND

A head is a terrible thing to lose, but a whole body is so much worse. The following are some of the most famous lost corpses. Maybe you can solve these mysteries . . .

NEFERTITI, QUEEN OF EGYPT

(c.1370 BC–c.1330 BC)

With such perfect cheekbones and one fabulously fancy hat,* Nefertiti was a legendary beauty one can't help but be itching to find. In 1898 three mummies were found in a secret chamber in the Valley of the Kings. Several Egyptologists later claimed that one of these mummies was Nefertiti. Clues indicating Nefertiti included: a first-class embalming job, a double-pierced left earlobe that matched a bust that was created of her head during her life, and a Nubian-style wig worn only by royals. DNA testing has so far been inconclusive because of the rampant inbreeding between Egyptian royals.** Other Egyptologists have concluded the mummies found were certainly royalty, but not necessarily Queen Nefertiti. So far the real Nefertiti has yet to be found.

---

*It is actually a crown, but I would totally wear this out of the house.
**It was common for brothers, sisters, and cousins to marry each other. This makes for one murky gene pool.

ALEXANDER THE GREAT, KING OF MACEDON *(356 BC–323 BC)*

If you are going to claim to be a god, then people of course are going to make a big fuss over you when you die. Alexander the Great told anyone who would listen that he was a descendant of Zeus-Ammon—the big cheese of Greek and Egyptian deities. You would think that would make him a tad invincible. Such was not the case. After a banquet, Alexander mysteriously died, possibly from poisoning.* His remains were encased in honey, and it was decided that a golden chariot would carry his casket from Mesopotamia to his burial location in Greece at Aegae. But Ptolemy Lagos, one of Alexander's generals, had other ideas. At the time, a popular prophecy alleged that whoever had Alexander's body would rule the world, so Ptolemy naturally wanted that voodoo magic on his side.

Legend has it that Ptolemy hijacked Alexander's hearse and had him buried in Alexandria, Egypt. In the following years, Alexander was molested by various emperors: Emperor Augustus (63 BC–AD 14) accidentally broke Alexander's nose off when he bent down to kiss the body, and Emperor Caracalla (AD 188–217) stole his silver shield to make himself invincible.

Oops!

---

*Malaria, typhoid, and alcohol poisoning have also been suspected causes.

Flash forward to AD 360, and Alexander's noseless body is subjected to a virtual phantasmagoria of disasters—wars, pillaging, riots, a few earthquakes, and one heck of a tsunami. During this time, the whereabouts of his tomb became lost (or destroyed). Some scholars still believe that Alexander's body is in Egypt, while others believe the body that was hijacked was actually a double, and the real Alexander is buried somewhere else. In September 2014, excavations began in Amphipolis in hopes of finding Alexander's tomb. Unfortunately, these excavations proved that this location most likely contained Alexander's friend Hephaestion.

GENGHIS KHAN, MONGOL LEADER *(c.1162–1227)*

I would love to tell you all about Genghis Khan's funeral, but it was such a wild party that no one survived it. On August 18, 1227, Khan died

from unknown causes, possibly from falling off his horse. His last wishes were for his body to be buried where no one could find it, but you know how people just love to talk about epic funerals. Unless . . . they can't. First, the two thousand people who attended his funeral were massacred. Then the eight hundred soldiers who had done the massacring were executed. Khan was supposedly placed in an unmarked grave, and a river was diverted to flow over the site, forever hiding it. Today Khan is worshipped as a national hero in Mongolia, but despite various researchers' efforts, the location of his tomb remains a mystery.

VLAD THE IMPALER, PRINCE OF WALLACHIA *(1431–1476/77)*

It seems like it might be a seriously bad idea to crack open the tomb of a five-hundred-year-old vampire. This has not stopped several historians from digging up tombs in monasteries to find Prince Vlad Tepes III— otherwise known as Vlad Dracula, whose name Bram Stoker borrowed for his novel *Dracula*. He was also called Vlad the Impaler, and he earned that nickname the hard-won way . . . some breathtakingly vicious torture. Let's see. Where shall we start? Well, there was the nailing his enemies' hats to their heads, chopping off various body parts (my favorite), and the always-creative impaling his enemies on a stake. Legend has it that his head was sent to Constantinople, and his body was buried at the Comana Monastery in modern-day Romania. While several tombs have been opened in the search, his remains have yet to be found.

ALBERT EINSTEIN

March 14, 1879–April 18, 1955

PICKING HIS BRAIN

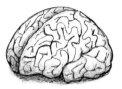

Albert Einstein didn't care much about his body parts. He ate greasy sausages and chocolate-covered ice cream cones that surely didn't help his heart. He smoked a big, smelly tobacco pipe every day that corroded his lungs. He had unruly, frizzy white hair—a look he claimed he got through "negligence." Even on a visit to the White House to meet with President Franklin Roosevelt, he couldn't bother to put socks on his feet. On most days, Einstein looked like he had been turned upside down on a wild roller-coaster ride and left there. And he made no apologies about it. He was far too busy solving physics's greatest mysteries to care about physical appearances. He once said, "It would be a sad situation if the wrapper were better than the meat wrapped inside it."

With such little concern for his "wrapper," it makes sense that Einstein told his biographer, "I want to be cremated so people don't come to worship at my bones." Always a private person, Einstein feared people would turn his body parts into relics, objects considered holy. It turns out, he was right to be concerned.

Einstein died in 1955 from a ruptured abdominal aneurysm. Per his wishes, his ashes were scattered in a secret location along the Delaware River. But earlier that morning . . . that was when things got dicey.

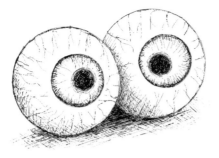

Very dicey. Einstein's body was pretty much carved up like a holiday turkey, with each of his doctors getting their favorite piece of meat. Einstein's warm brown eyes were scooped out and given to his eye doctor, Henry Adams. Adams stored them in a safe deposit box in New Jersey and took them out once or twice a year to sneak a peek at them.* Einstein's heart and liver went to a few medical students. No one knows where those bits ended up. They were last seen in a bucket in the Princeton Hospital.

Then there was the real prize—Einstein's brain. The brain went to Dr. Thomas Harvey, a pathologist described by those who knew him as "a real trippy dude." Harvey's job was to complete the autopsy report. He did complete that task. And then . . . he got a bit creative.

Let's start with the autopsy. On the morning of April 18, Harvey gently parted Einstein's white nimbus of hair, placed his chisel into an incision on the skull, whacked it with a mallet, and rocked the head back and forth until . . . voilà. Einstein's head split wide open.** Harvey then severed the cranial nerves and gently lifted out the gray, slippery brain matter or what Einstein had called his "laboratory." Then Harvey photographed the brain from different angles and sketched out different sections.

This was all standard autopsy stuff.

---

*Rumor has it that pop star Michael Jackson offered Adams several million dollars for Einstein's peepers, but Adams turned him down. You see, there is money to be made in body parts.
**Coincidently, this is the same technique used to crack open a coconut.

Then things got a bit wacky. Harvey must have found that his sketches were missing a certain artistic verve, so he hired a portrait painter named Anne Bonine Brower to create a still life of Einstein's brain.* But a painting didn't seem nearly enough to preserve such an important piece of history. So Harvey cut the brain into pieces ranging from the size of a turkey leg to a sugar cube and put them in a glass Mason jar.** He then took the brain home and stashed it behind a beer cooler.

Today people have mixed feelings on what Harvey did, probably because at one point he kept the brain in his sock drawer.*** Some see

him as a no-good, sticky-fingered crook who swiped the brain for his own ten seconds of fame. Harvey did not see it as theft. He saw himself as the guardian of science and the keeper of the brain's secrets.

It is understandable why Harvey wanted to save Einstein's brain. Einstein's brain had accomplished more in one year than most people's brains do in a lifetime. Oddly, it had a dubious start. Einstein was born in 1879, with a lopsided head that his grandmother said was "much too fat." He

---

*Brower was so excited to get the job that she didn't charge Harvey. She probably thought it would lead to more career opportunities. Sadly, Brower did not go on to paint more brains.
**I apologize for all the food references. I am writing this during lunch, and I am rather hungry.
***It kept his socks smelling fresh.

didn't speak until he was three, causing his parents to believe he was just *zurückgeblieben* (mentally challenged), He got mostly good grades at school but was always mocking his teachers behind their backs and cutting class. He was kind of a screw-up, so much so that he couldn't get a job after graduation. So he worked odd jobs, including a stint as a substitute teacher.

Eventually Einstein grew into his fat head. When he was twenty-three years old, he got a job as a patent clerk. Being a patent clerk was a pretty easy gig that allowed Einstein time for his "thought experiments." During one of these thought experiments, he wondered what it would

be like to travel on a beam of light. Three years later he made an important discovery: he determined that nothing could go faster than the speed of light (186,282 miles per second). If the speed of light acted as a cosmic speed limit, then mass—the amount of matter in an object—could turn into energy and energy could turn into mass. Einstein whittled it all down to one equation called the Theory of Relativity ($E = mc^2$). In Einstein's equation, the energy contained in an object (E) is equal to the mass of the object (m) multiplied by the speed of light (c) squared.

$$E = mc^2$$

If this all makes your head hurt, don't feel bad. At the height of Einstein's popularity, it was believed that only half the people in the United States understood $E = mc^2$.* Which is why Harvey saved Einstein's brain. He wanted to know what made Einstein tick. So over the years, Harvey sent slides of the brain to various neurologists to help him unlock those secrets. Most just thought he was daffy. A few did take him seriously.

In 2011 one research study found Einstein had something very unique going on between the left and right sides of his brain. People today think of themselves as either right- or left-brained in the same way that they are either right- or left-handed, but brains are much

---

*Probably fewer people do today.

more complicated than hands. When you solve a complex math problem or create an amazing piece of art, you are actually using both sides of your brain. Our left side controls logic, linear problem solving, and picking out details. The right side controls our intuition, creative problem solving, and big-picture thinking. For example, as you thoroughly immerse yourself in this book, the left side recognizes the words, but the right side gives them meaning.

Consequently, the real genius lies not in your left or right side of your brain but in the center. The center contains a dense network of fibers called the corpus callosum, which allows the right and left sides of the brain to work together. Think of it as the referee for your left and right brain thoughts.

Einstein's brain was different because it had one colossally large corpus callosum with twice the densely packed fibers of the average man of the same age.* These fibers acted as pathways between the right and the left sides of the brain. So while most

Corpus Callosum

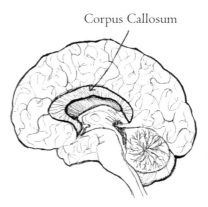

---

*Now, don't let this give you an Einstein fat head, but younger brains have far more connections in their corpus callosum than adult brains do. So the good news is that you can probably kick your parents' butts at memory or math problems, or any sort of creative task. The bad news is that if you don't use your brain, then all those wonderful connections in your corpus callosum start to die off and you become . . . well, average. I recommend rereading this book to prevent that from happening.

poor slobs have a few pathetic cow paths connecting the right and left sides, Einstein had one superhighway, Gordian knot of connections that allowed for more unique and brilliant thoughts.

Scientists today are still discovering new things about Einstein's brain. It may take years of peering down the lens of a microscope and conducting more research to truly understand why some people think differently.* Perhaps Einstein knew the true secret to genius when he said, "It's not that I'm so smart, it's just that I stay with problems longer."

Where are they now?

Harvey returned Einstein's brain to the National Museum of Health and Medicine. In 2013, slides of Einstein's brain went on display at the Mütter Museum in Philadelphia and became part of the museum's permanent collection. Scientists continue to hope that someday Einstein's brain might reveal its secrets.

---

*Okay, I am going to let you in on a little secret (which is why I put this in tiny print so adults might miss it). There are a lot of fancy-shmancy research papers being published every year on Einstein's brain, but the truth is this: we don't have a clue why he was so darn smart. The human brain is the most complex organ in the human body. Perhaps someday you will figure it out for the rest of us.

BITS ON BRAINS

ABRAHAM LINCOLN *(1809–1865)*

In the nineteenth century, people believed big brains meant you were smart, and little brains meant you might have trouble tying your shoes.

So of course, everyone was curious to see how Lincoln's brain would measure up. During his autopsy, Lincoln's physician removed the president's brain and recorded it as "not above the ordinary for a man of Lincoln's size." Unfortunately, he failed to record the actual weight. The average male brain weighs about three pounds. The female brain is 10 to 15 percent lighter. In reality, having a larger brain does not mean a person is smarter.*

EDGAR ALLAN POE *(1809–1849)*

Poe had a funny sort of brain. Sure, he was all dark and twisted with that creepy raven and one-eyed-black-cat stuff,** but his actual brain was a bit weird too . . . It was indestructible.

When Poe died, no one in Baltimore really cared. Ten or fewer people showed up for his funeral, and he wasn't even given a headstone. Twenty-six years later people

---

*If it did, then sperm whales with their seventeen-pound brains would rule the earth.
**If you don't know what I am talking about, just read "The Raven" or "The Black Cat" (after you are done reading this book, of course).

began to realize that Poe was a literary genius.* The people of Baltimore decided that they should at least move him to a proper grave. But when his coffin was opened, onlookers were surprised to see his brain was still intact even though the rest of his body had decomposed. Witnesses described it as "dried and hardened in the skull." Now, I know you paid attention to my heartfelt description of decomposition at the beginning of the book, so you already know that a brain is one of the first things to decay. Some historians believe that it was not a brain still rattling around in Poe's skull, but something far worse. Only a brain tumor would leave a hardened mass inside a skull.

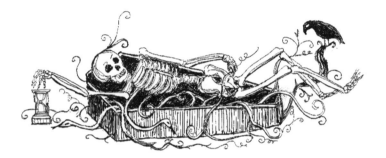

VOLTAIRE, FRENCH PHILOSOPHER *(1694–1778)*

His brain was cut out and carried home in a jam jar after his autopsy by his pharmacist. The location of his brain is unknown today.

VLADIMIR LENIN, COMMUNIST REVOLUTIONARY *(1870–1924)*

His brain has been sliced and diced and studied endlessly under microscopes. So far the conclusion has been that Lenin's brain is "nothing special."**

---

*People are funny like that.
**I would have to agree.

ELVIS PRESLEY

January 8, 1935–August 16, 1977

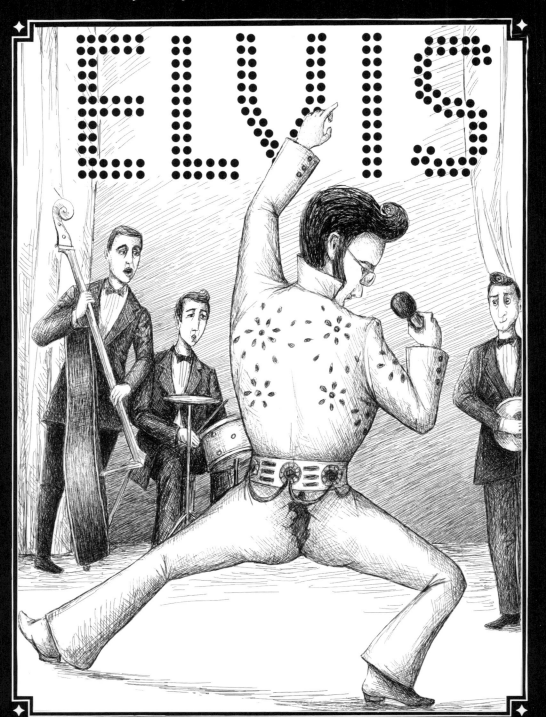

WARTS AND ALL

Every king needs a queen, even in the afterlife. For Elvis Presley, King of Rock 'n' Roll, that queen would be Joni Mabe—better known as Joni Mabe the Elvis Babe. Since Elvis's death, Mabe has collected more than thirty thousand items for her Panoramic Encyclopedia of Everything Elvis collection. The "Everything" part is no joke. Mabe has Elvis poodle skirts, an Elvis prayer rug, Elvis velvet paintings, and a vial of Elvis Sweat. She is particularly proud of her Maybe Elvis Toenail, found in 1983, embedded in one of the carpets of Elvis's Graceland home.* But the crown jewel to her queenly collection is one hunk, a hunk of burning wart.** During the height of Elvis mania in 1958, a military doctor removed the wart from the King's right wrist and had the good sense to save it. He later sold it to Mabe for an undisclosed amount. Now Mabe keeps her tiny, fleshy prize in a test tube filled with formaldehyde and nestled in a swath of red velvet.

Like most Elvis artifacts, everyday items have become worth far more in death than they ever were in life. The Americans for Cloning

---

*It's a big maybe, considering six hundred thousand tourists go through Graceland each year.
**In case you didn't get my bad pun, listen to Elvis's song "Burning Love." I promise that is my last bad Elvis pun. Maybe.

Elvis (yes, that is a real organization) offered to buy the wart in hopes of someday cloning Elvis. But Mabe would not part with her wart for any price.* She is against cloning Elvis for two reasons: First, it can't be done from the wart. A wart is caused by a virus. According to Mabe, if you tried to clone Elvis's wart, you would just end up with "a wart with maybe sideburns." Second, Mabe voiced the obvious trauma it would cause Elvis's clone: "I think it would be cruel to bring him back because he wouldn't have a mama. And he was really a mama's boy."

True enough. Elvis didn't grow up with much, but he did have his mother's love. He was born on January 8, 1935, in a small house in Tupelo, Mississippi, without running water or electricity. For a bathroom, his dad built an outhouse in the backyard—a hole in the ground flanked by four walls. Elvis did not have any brothers or sisters to fight him for time in this makeshift bathroom. His twin brother died when his mom gave birth to Elvis, and she could not have any more children.

In school, Elvis was a fairly good student and got Bs in math and English. In the eighth grade, he got a C− in music after his music teacher told him he couldn't

*Mabe really will not sell the wart to anyone. (Michael Jackson's attorney tried.) But she will sell you a T-shirt with the inscription THE KING IS GONE, BUT THE WART LIVES ON.

sing. Although mostly self-taught, Elvis believed he could sing. His teacher just didn't "appreciate his kind of singing." The problem was that Elvis did not sing like the other kids. He sounded a bit like a degenerate. At the time, Elvis's music could best be described as a mixture of rhythm and blues, country, and gospel. If you think your parents don't like your music now, you should have heard what 1950s parents said about Elvis and his "devil's music." You know it today as rock, but that word was not used until 1951, when Cleveland, Ohio, disc jockey Alan Freed coined the term rock and roll to describe up-tempo R&B music.

Elvis also didn't look like the other kids in high school. He wore pink shirts and a black bolero jacket to school like some sort of swanky bullfighter. He wore his long hair slicked back with Vaseline in ducktails and grew sideburns (unheard of at the time). He walked with a swagger, swiveled his hips when he sang, and had the kind of come-hither bedroom eyes that made parents want to lock up their daughters. Elvis was your typical bad boy.

Like most rebels, he wouldn't be told that he wasn't good enough. Throughout the fall of 1953, Elvis stopped by Sun Studios in Memphis looking for work as a backup singer. Elvis's first big break came when a band called the Starlite Wranglers was looking for a singer. Elvis auditioned and sang a bunch of songs, but it was his rendition of "That's All Right, Mama," a blues song by Arthur "Big Boy" Crudup, that won over record executives.* A few days later the song made its debut on a local radio station. As soon as Elvis's voice hit the airwaves, the station switchboard lit up with listeners asking for the song to be played again and again.

---

*Crudup's song was titled "That's All Right." Of course, Elvis added the "Mama" part.

Elvis skyrocketed to fame, eventually being called the King of Rock 'n' Roll. But like most young stars who rise so high, fame became a heavy crown to bear. Elvis had a nonstop schedule of movies, concerts, and interviews. He hung around a posse of boys that the press referred to as his Memphis Mafia. They wore black mohair suits, packed guns, and were always surrounded by beautiful girls.

Elvis tried to settle down and focus on his family. He married Priscilla Presley in 1967 and had a daughter named Lisa Marie in 1968. Elvis was a doting father and loved Priscilla, but he had a hard time juggling fans and family. In 1973 Priscilla and Elvis left a Memphis courtroom, hand in hand, their divorce finalized but obviously still caring for each other.

Elvis's motto had always been "The truth will set you free." Unfortunately, none of Elvis's friends were willing to tell Elvis the truth . . . He was spiraling out of control. As the demands of his career increased, he couldn't function without his Daddy's Little Helpers—a lethal cocktail of drugs, including amphetamines, sleeping  pills, LSD, Demerol, codeine, and the cherry on top . . . Dilaudid (synthetic heroin). His diet became the stuff of artery-clogging legends. Let's just say he really liked bacon: potatoes and bacon, biscuits and bacon, peanut butter and banana milk shakes with, yes, . . . bacon, and what he is best remembered for—fried peanut butter and banana bacon sandwiches. Soon he ballooned to more than three hundred pounds and was splitting his pants onstage. It wasn't kingly.

His unhealthy lifestyle and drug abuse eventually caught up to him. On August 16, 1977, the King of Rock was found dead on the floor of his bathroom beside his throne (the porcelain one). The cause of death was "cardiac arrhythmia," but that may have been a polite way of saying he had popped his last pill.*

More than fifty thousand mourners attended his funeral, and some people could not accept he was gone. According to the Elvis Sighting Society (yes, that is a real organization), he has been spotted in a burger joint in Kalamazoo, Michigan; in a coffee shop in Tweed, Ontario; and may have become a federal secret agent for the US government.** When Joni Mabe is asked if she believes Elvis might still be alive, she replies with absolute conviction, "If he was, he would come see me." Like most fans, Mabe can't help falling in love with Elvis. I guess you could say that she loves her king . . . warts and all.***

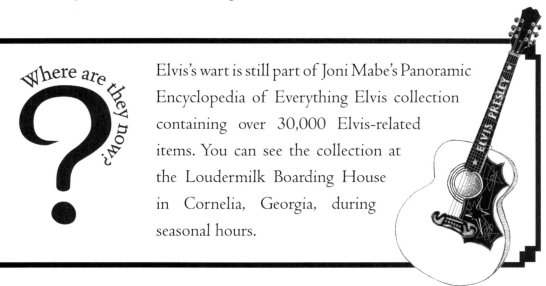

Where are they now?

Elvis's wart is still part of Joni Mabe's Panoramic Encyclopedia of Everything Elvis collection containing over 30,000 Elvis-related items. You can see the collection at the Loudermilk Boarding House in Cornelia, Georgia, during seasonal hours.

---

*Some medical professionals believe Elvis's death was caused by an enlarged colon that caused life-threatening constipation. Basically, Elvis died straining to go to the bathroom.

**If you spot Elvis, please call the Elvis Sighting Hotline.

***I so lied about refraining from bad Elvis puns. Really, I have no self-control. If this does not get cut, please blame my editor.

CLONING BODY PARTS

Cloning Elvis's bits might not be too far off. The process of creating a healthy liver, heart, or skin from a person's DNA is called therapeutic cloning. During therapeutic cloning, the nucleus, or brain, of the cell is inserted into a fertilized egg whose nucleus has been removed. The egg then divides several times and forms an embryo, similar to how you developed inside your mother. But instead of the embryo implanting into a mother's uterus, special cells are removed and harvested in a petri dish. These special cells are called stem cells, and they are the building blocks for your body because, once they start dividing, they can become the basis for any cell in your body—heart cells, muscle cells, liver cells, skin cells, etc. Scientists are hoping to someday be able to coax these stem cells into becoming different body parts. Cloning organs would be a tremendous medical advancement. A sick person might not reject a cloned organ since it is genetically identical to the original organ, unlike

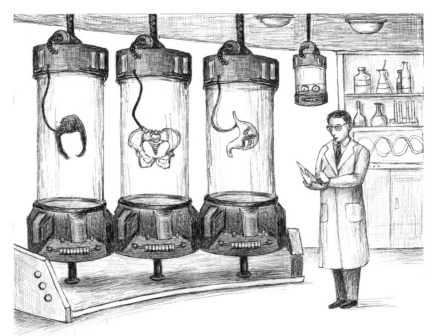

a donated heart or kidney. Scientists have already been successful in making bladders from stem cells, so cloning Elvis's sideburns might someday be possible.

A more dubious method of cloning is through cryonics. Cryonics is the technique used to store human heads at extremely low temperatures with the hope of one day reviving them or as the cryonics folk call it "reanimating" them. The belief is that people will eventually be brought back to life through stem cell regrowth. Think of it like having a Chia Pet, except instead of growing vegetation hair, you would sprout a new body from your head.

The process goes like this: Your head is packed in ice and injected with heparin (an anticoagulant) to prevent your blood from clotting. Unfortunately, freezing a head isn't like, say, freezing meatballs. Your body has cells that are filled with water, and when you freeze them, the cell membranes burst. This means that once you are unthawed, you would get all mushy. So, to keep the head cool without reaching a freezing point, the liquid in your cells is replaced with a glycerol-based chemical cocktail. Then your head is stored upside down in a large metal tank called a cryostat and filled with liquid nitrogen to keep it at constant low temperatures.

One of the most famous examples of cryonics is baseball legend Theodore Samuel "Ted" Williams. After he died in 2002, Ted's head was cryogenically frozen, per his son's instructions. This resulted in a firestorm of complaints from fans and loved ones who felt that the baseball legend never wanted his head saved. Maybe someday Ted will "reanimate" and tell us what he thought of the debacle.

RECYCLING BITS
FIRST STEPS

I have said throughout this book that there is money to be made from body parts. Let this be your guide. First step: it is really rude to steal a body part if the person is not dead yet. It may seem like a no-brainer, but in the past, humans have not always done such a great job determining whether someone was really dead. Sure, if the body was all black and smelly, that was a pretty good indicator that the jig was up, but what if someone had recently died? In the nineteenth century, doctors would typically feel a wrist for a pulse, place an ear against the chest to listen for a heartbeat, or place a mirror under the deceased's mouth to see if the glass fogged up with breath. These techniques worked splendidly, unless someone had fallen into a coma—a state of unconsciousness that makes someone appear lifeless. Then things got dicey. Doctors called comas "death trances" because they believed the person was simply in a deep sleep. To avoid premature burials, the medical community devised some clever ways to determine if someone was really, really dead.

TORTURE

One way to make someone sit up and behave was to beat the snot out of him. Feet were burned, fingers dislocated, tongues pulled, and bodies were even beheaded. Another method was pouring scalding hot water over a body, which surely must have led to some crispy not-so-dead patients.

WAIT IT OUT

Sometimes "dead houses" were used. This is just as scary as it sounds. Dead houses were buildings to store dead people until the body putrefied—a sure sign that you were really, really dead.

SAVED BY THE BELL

Sometimes the insides of closed coffins were rigged with ropes that could be pulled to ring a bell on the outside of the coffin. These pulley-and-bell contraptions alerted the night watchman that someone had awoken from a deathly slumber. It is from this practice that we get the saying "Saved by the bell."

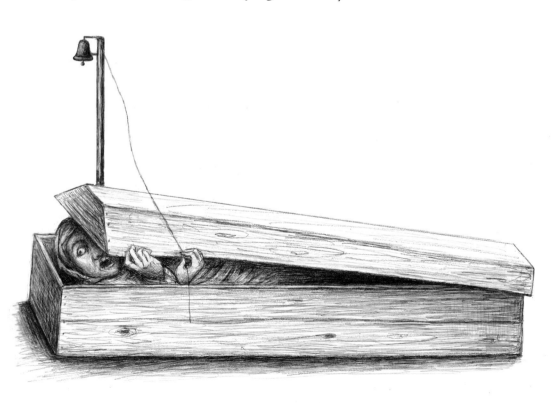

A HAPPILY EVER AFTERLIFE

Before collecting any body part, it's important to exhaust every method that might bring a person back to life. Here are a few of the past's favorite methods.

SHOCK THEM TO LIFE!

If there was one way to make someone sit up and pay attention (alive or dead), it was galvanism. Galvanism used an electric current to make the muscles of the body contract. It got its name from its inventor, Luigi Galvani, who experimented with using electrical currents on dissected frogs. If watching dead frog legs twitch was amusing, we can imagine the hours of fun Italian scientist Giovanni Aldini had when he did the same thing to dead people. In 1803 Aldini demonstrated the powers of electricity to a London audience when he applied electrodes to the body of executed criminal George Forster. When George's eyes popped open in one shocking look of surprise, spectators began to wonder about the possibilities of electricity bringing the dead back to life. (It didn't work for George, but it did cause some scary twitching.) Legend has it that these spooky demonstrations led one writer named Mary Wollstonecraft Shelley to write a gothic novel about such a monster reanimated by a wacky scientist. She named her monster Frankenstein.

But using electricity to bring people back to life is not as crazy as it sounds. Doctors today use an electrical device called a defibrillator to to interrupt the irregular heart rhythms of people having heart attacks. Each year defibrillators have the potential to save more than one hundred thousand lives (if available), and no one looks like Frankenstein when they come back to life.

OUT LIKE A LAMB

A day after George Washington died (p. 31), one of his physicians arrived and claimed he could revive the late president by transfusing him with lamb's blood. The belief was that lamb's blood had a special vitality that could reanimate the body. George's family decided to let him rest in peace instead.

PLAY INNOCENT, NOT DEAD

In the sixteenth century, it was believed that a dead murder victim would bleed in front of his murderer. In 1572 England, Ann Crockett requested that her murdered husband's body be brought before the accused because she believed that her husband's wounds would bleed afresh. Unfortunately, the coroner conducting the case was married to the sister of the accused. Fearing incriminating blood, he refused the wife's request.*

---

*Curiously, the coroner's report also stated that the fatal head wound was due to the natural shape of the deceased's head.

THE MOST WANTED

The following body parts were the most profitable bits to collect.

LUCKY FINGERS

In sixteenth-century Germany, an executed criminal's finger was often stolen because it was believed to bring good fortune. Sort of like a lucky rabbit's foot . . . except it was from a very unlucky dead person.

BITE THE DUST

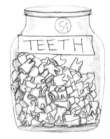

In the days before modern dentistry, no one really bothered to brush their teeth, so missing teeth became pretty common. Need a new set of chompers? No worries. Just steal some from the dead. (See chapter on George Washington, p. 26.) In 800 BC in Etruria (central Italy), corpse teeth were removed and used in dentures for wealthy people. In the eighteenth and nineteenth centuries, teeth were stolen from soldiers who had died on the battlefield. These dentures became known as Waterloo teeth, named after the Battle of Waterloo.

GIVE 'EM THE BOOT

After a criminal was hanged, his skin was sometimes tanned and made into anything that needed sturdy material—belts, bags, boots, and fancy book covers. In 1881 outlaw George Parrott was arrested for killing two police officers. After he was hanged, his skin was made into boots and a medical bag.

WIGGING OUT

Hair was often plundered as souvenirs and saved in lockets (see chapter on Beethoven). In the eighteenth century, hair was used to make fine wigs. (This led to a lot of head scratching when lice came along for the ride.) Not to be outdone in the recycling department, the Victorians wove their dead relatives' hair into "hair jewelry."

NOT RIGHT IN THE HEAD

What can you do if you find a random skull in your garden? If you are Romantic poet Lord Byron, you might think—hmmm, it's round, it's hollow, and it's creepy . . . Why, I could polish it

up and drink out of it! When writer Nathaniel Hawthorne visited Lord Byron's house years after Byron had died, he peeked inside the cabinet and found the ghoulish goblet. Hawthorne couldn't help but remark, "A man must be either very drunk or very thirsty, before he would taste wine out of such a goblet."*

---

*Tip: if you want to drink from a skull, you must drink from the back of the skull or the liquid will fall out of the eye sockets and wreck your shirt. How I know this is beyond the scope of this book.

CORPSE MEDICINE

By now you probably know that body parts were saved for a whole slew of reasons, but one of the most common was to cure illnesses.*

A SPOONFUL OF SUGAR . . .

If the saying holds true that you are what you eat, then this bit of corpse medicine is one sweet cure. In twelfth-century Arabia, when

an old man was nearing his final days, he would be instructed to eat only honey and bathe in honey. And I mean . . . only honey. After a month of this treatment, he would eventually die.** Then he would be placed in a stone coffin full of . . . you guessed it, more honey. After a hundred years, the man's coffin would be popped open like fine wine, except with sticky bits. The honeyed corpse goop would then be scooped out and used to cure broken legs and wounds. It sounds crazy, but honey does actually cure wounds by drawing out water and disinfecting.

LOVE YOUR MUMMY

In the sixteenth century, doctors believed the corpses of holy people had

---

*The legal department wants me to let you know that none of these cures should be practiced without adult supervision.

**Because, yes, sugar is bad for you.

magical powers. To cure Don Carlos, Prince of Austria, of a head wound, doctors placed a hundred-year-old mummy of the holy man Fray Diego in Don Carlos's bed. Doctors believed it worked because Don Carlos got better.

Mummies were also ground up and made into powder to make people stronger. Sixteenth-century King Francis I of France ate a pinch of mummy every day with rhubarb.

FAT AND HAPPY

In the seventeenth century, the local executioner hanged criminals by day and sold their bits by night. One of the most profitable body parts was human fat. It was rubbed on wounds and also used to make candles and soap.

THE KING'S DROPS

King Charles II of England (1630–1685) had a secret feel-good remedy called the King's Drops. He even had his own laboratory for mixing up his pills and potions. What was in the secret sauce? Powdered skull.

A HAREBRAINED IDEA

In the seventeenth century, distilled brains became the cure-all for head pains. German chemist Johann Schröder recorded recipes that included grinding up the brain of a young man "who died violently" into a pulp and then mixing it with a floral concoction of peonies, black cherry blossoms, lavender, and lilies. Schröder was also helpful enough to add recipe substitutions. If one could not find a young man's brain, then an elk's brain would work quite nicely.

BAD BLOOD

In Ancient Rome, once a gladiator fell to his death, his blood became a valuable medicine. Wealthy aristocrats would pay to suck the blood straight from a fallen gladiator's vein. It was used mostly to treat epilepsy but also to increase energy.

In medieval times, the executioner could make a quick buck by selling an executed criminal's blood. It was believed that drinking a criminal's blood would make you stronger. People would drink it hot and fresh right off the scaffold, like they were licking up tomato soup.*

Blood as a cure-all continued to be used well into the fifteenth century. When Pope Innocent VIII fell gravely ill in 1492, his doctors prescribed drinking blood from

---

*As always . . . apologies for the food reference, but this tomato soup I am eating is simply delicious.

three boys. It didn't work. The pope died, and so did the boys who were bled to death.*

Using blood as medicine continued into the eighteenth century. When Louis XVI was sent to the guillotine in 1793, the crowds rushed toward the scaffold to dip their handkerchiefs in his royal blood. It was believed that a king's blood was especially potent to bring good health.

BATHING BEAUTIES

When king or gladiator blood wasn't available, a young girl's blood could do wonders for your complexion. One of the most notorious blood lovers was German countess Elizabeth Bathory. In 1610 Elizabeth was arrested for torturing and killing more than sixty servant girls. Legend has it that after she slaughtered the girls, she bathed in their blood to stay youthful.**

---

*Pope Innocent VIII is best remembered for fathering sixteen illegitimate children, endorsing slavery, and giving his stamp of approval on the witch hunts that led to thousands of women hanged for witchcraft. Obviously, drinking blood was just a typical day on the job.

**Small print that wrecks all my fun: the murders were corroborated by more than three hundred witnesses, but accounts of the blood bubble baths were recorded years after her death and never came forth in her trial.

DEATHLY DECOR

Sarah Bernhardt was definitely onto something when she used a coffin as a bed and a skull as a letter holder. Sometimes a few funeral trimmings and body parts can really liven up a place.

HOUSE OF DEATH

Nothing says death and decay like a charnel house. A charnel house, or ossuary, is a great big house decorated with human bones. It's always tough to pick your favorite ossuary, but I have to go with the Sedlec Ossuary located in the Czech Republic. (The chandelier made from bones really makes it stand out.) Known as the Bone Church, Sedlec was founded

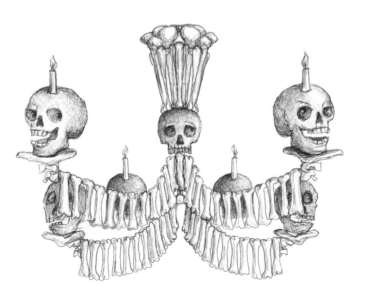

in the thirteenth century when Abbot Henry brought some "holy soil" back from Jerusalem and scattered it on Sedlec Cemetery. Obviously, everyone wanted to be buried in holy soil instead of just plain old dirt. Soon there were so many bones they had to be moved inside to the crypt. And let's face it . . . if you are going to go through the trouble of moving a large pelvic bone, you might as well turn it into a wall hanging.

THE BRIGHTEST MINDS

In eighteenth-century Paris, it became the custom among aristocratic ladies to use a skull decorated with ribbons as a candle holder. Queen Marie-Catherine Leszczyńska (1703–1768) lighted her way with the skull of author and famed beauty Ninon de l'Enclos (1620–1705).

SWEET DREAMS

In the seventeenth century, an order of Roman nuns called the Sepolta Viva, or "Buried Alive" sisters, would bid one another sweet dreams every night with the words: "Remember, sister, we all have to die." Turns out they really meant it. They slept in coffins instead of beds.

EMPIRE OF THE DEAD

In a charming area of Paris known as the Les Halles neighborhood, you won't find any tall buildings. Buildings greater than a certain height cannot be built in this area since the foundation is too weak, because underneath those picturesque shops and cafés lies an underground world of long, dark tunnels made entirely of bones. Known as the Empire of the Dead, the bones are the remains of six million Parisians. The bones were transferred underground in 1780 after Paris's cemeteries became too overcrowded. Today curious tourists can visit the Empire of the Dead. Just try not to get lost and become part of the structure.

DEAD-END JOBS

With all this talk of body parts, you must be dying to pursue a career with the dead. Here are a few morbid career opportunities.

A SAD JOB

Acting is not the only profession where a flair for the dramatic comes in handy. If you can cry on cue, you might want to consider a career as a professional funeral mourner, called a moirologist. The profession originated around 156 BC in China. Moirologists were basically paid to show up at funerals and bawl  their eyes out. This made the deceased look missed and took the pressure off the family to shed tears. The practice continues today in China and the Middle East and has gained popularity with the always "Keep Calm and Carry On" British. For forty-five pounds an hour (about seventy-seven US dollars), professional mourners are paid to show up at a funeral wearing black and weeping their hearts out.

IT'S ALL FUN AND GAMES AT A ROMAN FUNERAL

While some cultures need a few tears to make a funeral more entertaining, the Romans preferred a little bloodshed to liven things up. The Romans believed human sacrifices honored the dead, but just butchering someone seemed so senseless. Instead they staged elaborate games where armed men called gladiators would combat, sometimes to the death. These gladiator funeral games became such a popular way to honor the deceased that by 175 BC, it was considered entirely uncouth to throw a funeral without having someone die at it.

As funeral gladiator games got more and more lavish, one fortunate person called an editor got the job of organizing the events. These event coordinators were not the lovable editors of today who make books so darn special. These editors were responsible for making sure the bloodbaths stayed entertaining. Editors on top of their game would pit gladiatrix (female gladiators) against one another, or slaughter a few giraffes.*

Your editor wants more bloodshed!

---

*Slaughtering giraffes is not nearly as cruel as cutting out precious words. (If this makes it into the book, then my editor does not read small print.)

By 105 BC, Romans so enjoyed the gladiator games that they didn't really feel they needed a funeral to have them. Eventually the games had very little to do with honoring the dead and more to do with watching fighting dwarfs maul each other. Unfortunately, this was a truly dead-end job. The typical gladiator lived only to his early twenties.

But if watching people battle to the death at a funeral doesn't make you realize just how sick and twisted the Romans really were, then maybe funeral clowns will convince you. During Roman funerals, clowns would dress in masks and dance around the coffin. These merry mourners were hired to lighten the funeral gloom by cracking jokes and trying to make people laugh.*

HANGERS-ON

In the movies, they make your typical hanging look so effortless. Sadly, hanging in medieval times was not your quick-and-painless death. In fact, it could take up to an hour. Fortunately, a "hanger-on" was allowed

---

*Let's just get this out of the way now. While a book about dismembered body parts is positively hilarious, grown men wearing creepy masks and scaring the bejeezus out of innocent children is fundamentally disturbing.

to literally hang on to the condemned to speed up his death. Today the word "hanger-on" refers to someone who hangs on to another person for his own personal gain.

SEARCHING FOR DEATH

Let's face it. Medieval life wasn't all unicorns and fair maidens. With life expectancy around thirty-five years (less if you were poorer), death was lurking behind every corner and sometimes . . . right behind your neighbors' front door. That's where searchers of the dead came in handy. A searcher was an old woman who was responsible for going inside a house to determine the cause of death—usually plague.* 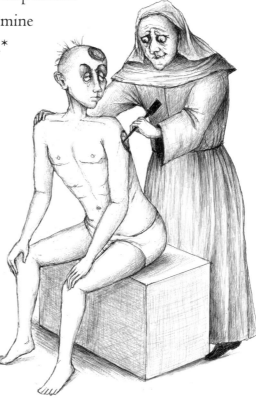 Searchers would examine the bodies and look for blackened skin and the telltale buboes—puss-filled sores exploding in the armpits. If plague was pronounced as the cause of death, the door would be marked with a painted cross, and the inhabitants would be quarantined inside the house for forty days. Since no one wanted to be stuck inside a plague house, this led to a lot of searchers being bribed to fudge death certificates.

---

*You know why this is in small print . . . I am about to tell you something about old people. You see, old people were just scary in medieval times. If you lived past thirty-five, you most likely were a witch. If you were old enough to repeatedly dodge the plague . . . well, you had to be a freak of nature.

EXECUTIONER

Job Requirements: Good aim swinging an ax, even with only two tiny holes to see through.

Benefits: You get to sell the blood and fat of dead people for extra cash.

Disadvantages: No one likes you. That is why you are wearing a mask.

Executioners were usually not your fine, upstanding citizens. They were often ex-criminals or deadbeats without many job prospects. That was because no one wanted the job. Sure, swinging an ax looked fun,

but it also required an amazing amount of strength and skill to chop off a head without making a mess.*

One of the most famous executioners was a fellow named Jack Ketch, who became England's official executioner in 1663. While most people are remembered for being really great at their jobs, Ketch is remembered because he was simply the worst executioner ever. He botched execution after execution, never quite getting the job done with one swing. His most bungled execution occurred in 1685 when he took eight swings to execute James Scott, Duke of Monmouth. Today British mothers still warn misbehaving children that Jack Ketch is going to get them.**

---

*Just trust me on this one.

**This only works on British children.

TIME TO FEED THE MAGGOTS

Ah . . . maggots. They grow up so darn fast. Their life cycles are informative to forensic entomologists because they indicate how long a person has been dead. For example, if a body has mature larvae feeding on it, then that person has been dead for approximately three weeks—the length of time for a maggot to go from egg to adult. After the maggot is  done feeding, it moves to a drier spot (sans juicy body), forms a cocoon, and . . . voilà, out pops a bouncing baby fly. A forensic entomologist is responsible for studying the life cycle of maggots and other bugs on corpses to determine the time and location of a death. One such case occurred on March 13, 1936, when Dr. Buck Ruxton was found guilty of killing his wife. He might have gotten away with the crime if it had not been for one piece of evidence—the maggots. Insect expert Dr. A. G. Mearns determined the date of death by the bluebottle larvae feeding on the body. (The maggots were twelve to fourteen days old.) This evidence corroborated with sightings of the doctor near where the body had been dumped on the suspected date of death.

DINING WITH THE DEAD

People tend to feel guilty about all sorts of things. Thankfully, nineteenth-century mourners had an ingenious way to absolve a dead person of any sins. At many rural funerals, a hard bread called a dead cake would be placed on the breast of the dearly departed. It was then the job of the sin eater to eat the bread off the corpse, thereby ingesting the deceased's sins.

UNLOVED BITS

So far we have covered hearts, heads, skulls, brains, fingers, legs, ears, hair, a token wart, and entire bodies. But some body parts never get the respect they deserve. This final bit is for those forgotten body parts.

THE UNAPPRECIATED COLON

Let's start with the unsung hero of the digestive track, the colon. In the eighteenth and nineteenth centuries, anatomy instructors would

wax poetic about the heart, lungs, and brain, but cut out the colon and throw it away. No one wanted to even talk about the poor colon.* Today you won't find a lot of colons lovingly saved in jars. However, you can take a trip to the Mütter Museum in Philadelphia to see the fabulously large colon that once belonged to J. W. When stretched out, the colon measures more than eight feet long with a circumference of twenty-seven inches. (The average colon is only four to five feet long.) J. W. suffered from Hirschsprung's disease, a congenital disease in which the nerve supply is missing in parts of the colon. As a result, the muscles to the colon do not contract, stool builds up, and the colon becomes

---

*If you think breaking wind can clear a room, you should see what removing a colon from a dead person can do. The colon contains noxious gases and undigested waste—not exactly enjoyable smells for watching an anatomy lesson.

more and more enlarged. Eventually the pressure on the walls of the colon causes decreased blood flow that can lead to fatal infections. (Think of squeezing a tube of toothpaste with the cap still on it.) Such was the fate of J. W., who was found dead on the floor of his bathroom at the age of twenty-nine.* His brown, leathery colon lives on and can be admired for the price of admission to the Mütter Museum.

TALKING TONSIL TRASH

More than five hundred thousand surgeries to remove tonsils are performed each year. Out of all those surgeries, thousands of parents ask all the same logical questions: What are the side effects? How long will it take to heal? And the obvious, will it hurt? But no one ever bothers to ask the most important question of all—what happens to the lopped-off tonsils? Well, if you have ever had your tonsils removed, you might have wondered the same thing. Sorry, no one is saving them.** According to the Medical Waste Tracking Act of 1988, tonsils are considered "potentially infectious" material and must be disposed of correctly. In most states, surgeons dispose of them in what's called a red bag.

This sure beats what happened in the past, when medical waste was just thrown out, only to sometimes later wash up on East Coast beaches.

---

*Some medical professionals believed Elvis also suffered from Hirschsprung's disease, which ultimately led to his death.

**When my son had a tonsillectomy, I almost asked to save the tonsils, but then thought better of it. I considered it "research." Others might not have seen it that way.

Thomas Alva Edison

February 11, 1847–October 18, 1931

LAST GASPS

Agreat biography breathes life into a person. But sometimes we need more. Sometimes it helps to see their actual breath. Fortunately, you can see inventor Thomas Edison's last breath captured in a glass test tube.

Thomas Alva Edison's first breath was in Milan, Ohio, on February 11, 1847. His family called him Al. His teachers called him "addled," which is a not-so-nice way of saying that little Al was confused. Somewhat crazy . . . yes. Confused . . . well, Edison never let questions go unanswered. As a child, he performed many experiments. He once sat on some eggs to see if he could make them hatch. They didn't, and the goose that laid them surely must have been annoyed. After observing birds, he wondered if their diet of fresh worms helped them fly. The only way to find out was to mash up some worms and feed them to a neighborhood girl. Obviously. She never got off the ground, but she did get rather sick. Edison was constantly experimenting, and those experiments led to some of our most important inventions: the phonograph, the motion picture, and what he is most remembered for, the incandescent lightbulb.

Edison lived in a world without electric light. In the nineteenth century, people used candles and gas lamps, which were expensive, not very bright, and covered the walls with thick soot. Luckily, Edison would change all that. He did not invent the lightbulb, but through his experiments with carbon filaments (the material inside a bulb), he was able to create incandescent lightbulbs that were cheaper and lasted longer.

Edison was constantly coming up with ideas and inventions. His desk contained a cubbyhole he labeled NEW THINGS. He spent many days at his lab at Menlo Park, New Jersey, mixing chemicals and tinkering with his phonograph. Sometimes he worked so hard he rarely slept. He would curl up in crumpled clothes on the workbench in his lab, sleep for a couple of hours, and then get up to work again. He once said: "Genius is one percent inspiration and ninety-nine percent perspiration."

Edison's hard work paid off. He earned 1,093 United States patents—a record that still stands today. People throughout America  admired him for his unique inventions and called him the Wizard of Menlo Park. But probably no one admired him more than his BFF, Henry Ford. Ford met Edison in 1896 when Ford worked as an engineer for the Edison Illuminating Company. The two met again sixteen years later and became inseparable as soon as they exchanged inventors' jokes. Ford was an industrialist and the first person to use the assembly line in his automobile plants. An assembly line is a way of breaking up the manufacturing process into stations where each person or machine is responsible for adding a different part to

the process. The assembly line allowed cars to be made faster and more cheaply, thereby allowing more families to afford one. Ford and Edison had many long conversations about someday building an electric car together, an invention well before their time.

It wasn't long before the two geniuses were camping together in the Florida Everglades. During these camping trips, they engaged in such manly competitions as tree chopping, sprinting, hunting, and "high kicking."* And, yes, a high-kicking contest is exactly what it sounds like—seeing who can kick the highest.** Ford became so close to Edison that in 1916 he purchased the house next to Edison's in Fort Myers, Florida. A wooden gate called the Friendship Gate separated the two houses but always remained open. Later in life, after Edison was

---

*Ford and Edison called themselves the "vagabonds," but if you look at the surviving film footage you get a very different picture of what they considered roughing it. They climbed trees in suits, had meals cooked by chefs, and had maids change the linens inside their gleaming white tents embroidered with their names.
**For the record, Edison outkicked Ford by seven inches.

confined to a wheelchair, Ford bought his own wheelchair so the two could race around the property together. Their friendship would last until Edison's death in 1931.

When those final moments came, Edison's son Charles took a test tube near the bedside and held it beneath his father's lips. Then when Edison breathed his last breath into the tube, Charles sealed it with paraffin wax. Knowing the deep respect Ford had for his father, he sent the test tube to Ford. Edison's last breath must have made Ford feel connected to his friend well after he lost him.

Edison believed there was an invisible electrical energy that linked the dead with the living. To bridge the gap, he worked on a "ghost box," which he described as "an apparatus to see if it is possible for personalities which have left this earth to communicate with us."

"It's very beautiful over there."
—Thomas Edison's last words

Some of Edison's ideas were a bit whacked, but he was correct about one thing—whether you choose to save a handwritten letter or an actual hand, the dead can reach out to the living. They reach out in the stories we choose to remember.*

THE END
(BUT NEVER REALLY)

 The test tube containing Edison's last breath can be found at the Henry Ford Museum in Dearborn, Michigan.

---

*Final note to the reader: I am not advocating saving Grandma's head in a jar to remember her, but it does certainly make for a great story.

ACKNOWLEDGMENTS

This book would not have been possible without a few people who kept all my body parts in place.

To Israel, who kept my heart in place.

To Alison, who kept my funny bone in place.

To my agent, Abigail Samoun, who kept my eyes in place and focused on completion.

To John, whose support kept me from losing my head.

To my children, Johnny and Charlotte, who kept my feet firmly planted on the ground.

To my parents, for everything, especially since they made my parts.

To my GI doctors of Massachusetts General Hospital, who saved my persnickety colon and tolerated my jokes about saving my intestines in a jar.

And lastly, to Sarah and everyone at Bloomsbury, who kept all the parts together and stayed committed to this book.

NOTES ON SOURCES

p. 6: "cry out with grief like an ocean raging with storm"
DuTemple, A. Lesley. *The Taj Mahal.* Minneapolis: Lerner, 2003, 11.

p. 8: "Death is the veil which those who live call life."
Shelley, Percy Bysshe. *The Poetical Works of P. B. Shelley.* London: C. Daly, 1839, 320.

p. 23: "I have eaten many strange things in my lifetime, but I have never eaten the heart of a king."
Murphy, Edwin. *After the Funeral: The Posthumous Adventures of Famous Corpses.* New York: Carol, 1995, 64.

p. 24: "tingling"
Freedman, David H. "20 Things You Didn't Know About Autopsies." *Discovery,* September 2012, 72.

p. 27: "the leaves shook on the tree"
Ferling, John. *The Ascent of George Washington: The Hidden Political Genius of an American Icon.* New York: Bloomsbury, 2010, 179.

p. 30: "are very troublesome to me at times"
Writings of Washington. Archive.org. https://archive.org/stream/writingsofgeorge26wash /writingsofgeorge26wash_djvu.txt. Accessed online on June 5, 2013.

p. 31: "'Tis well."
Betts, William W., Jr. *The Nine Lives of George Washington.* Bloomington, IN: iUniverse, 2013, 145.

p. 35: "it was already quite green"
"Hunting Haydn's Head," BBC Radio 4 broadcast by Simon Townley. http://www.bbc.co.uk /programmes/b00kmgrx. Accessed online on May 2009.

p. 36: "crowing like a cock"
Geiringer, Karl, with Irene Geiringer. *Haydn: A Creative Life in Music.* Berkeley: University of California Press, 1982, 24.

p. 43: "utterly untamed"
Lockwood, Lewis. *Beethoven: The Music and the Life.* New York: W. W. Norton, 2005, 492.

p. 45: "Applaud, friends, the comedy is finished."
Martin, Russell. *Beethoven's Hair: An Extraordinary Historical Odyssey and a Scientific Mystery Solved.* New York: Broadway Books, 2000, 252.

p. 47: "As soon as I am dead, if Dr. Schmidt is still alive, ask him in my name to describe my malady . . . so that so far as it is possible at least the world may become reconciled to me after my death."
Dickey, Colin. *Cranioklepty: Grave Robbing and the Search for Genius.* Lakewood, CO: Unbridled Books, 2010, 96.

p. 51: "The president. He was killed by an assassin."
Guelzo, Allen C. *Fateful Lightning: A New History of the Civil War and Reconstruction.* New York: Oxford
   University Press, 2012, 466.

p. 54: "boss body snatcher of Chicago"
Craughwell, Thomas J. *Stealing Lincoln's Body.* Cambridge, MA: Harvard University Press, 2007, 91.

p. 57: "somewhat shrunken"
Ibid., 179.

p. 71: "teacupful of brains"
Stabbed in the Brain: Phineas Gage. https://www.youtube.com/watch?v=FrULrWRlGBA.
   Accessed online on May 6, 2014.

p. 71: "a fungus"
Macmillan, Malcolm. *An Odd Kind of Fame: Stories of Phineas Gage.* Cambridge, MA: MIT Press,
   2000, 53.

p. 71: "No longer Gage."
Fleishchman, John. *Phineas Gage: A Gruesome but True Story about Brain Science.* Boston: Houghton
   Mifflin, 2002, 59.

p. 75: "Another way to take up more space"
Warhol, Andy. *The Philosophy of Andy Warhol (From A to B and Back Again).* Orlando: Harcourt, 2006, 50.

p. 75: "Dracula will never end."
Skal, J. David. *Bela Lugosi, Hollywood's Dark Prince.* Biography Channel. Oct. 1995.

p. 77: "the most handsome man on the American stage"
Nottingham, Theodore J. *The Curse of Cain: The Untold Story of John Wilkes Booth.* Newbury, West
   Berkshire, UK: Sovereign, 1998, 149.

p. 78: "Providence"
Impeachment investigation: Testimony taken before the Judiciary committee of the United States.
   39th Congress, 2d session, 1866–67. House, United States. 40th Congress, 1st session, 1867.

p. 79: "a straight fracture of the tibia about two inches above the ankle"
Samuel Mudd Statement, April 21, 1865, Assassination and Trial Papers.

p. 80: "right limb was greatly contused and perfectly black from a fracture of one of the long bones"
Guttridge, Leonard F. "Identification and Autopsy of John Wilkes Booth: Reexamining the
   Evidence." *Navy Medicine,* January-February 1993, p. 24.

p. 81: "painful imbecility"
Lincoln. Abraham. *Selections from the Writings of Abraham Lincoln.* New York: Scott, Foresman, 1922, 19.

p. 82: "lump of foul deformity"
Shakespeare, William. *Richard III,* act 1, scene 2.

p. 85: "We never actually lost the leg. It was just forgotten."
Johnson, Michael. "Sarah Bernhardt's Leg." *New York Times*, February 2, 2009.

p. 86: "It is you who have killed me!"
Gold, Arthur, and Robert Fizdale. *The Divine Sarah: A Life of Sarah Bernhardt*. New York: Knopf, 1991, 121.

p. 89: "The tear which you drew from me belongs to you. I place it at your feet."
Ibid., 140.

p. 90: "So happy my leg is cut off tomorrow."
Gottlieb, Robert. *Sarah: The Life of Sarah Bernhardt*. New Haven: Yale University Press, 2010, 167.

p. 90: "If it's my right leg you want, see the doctors; if it's the left leg, see my manager in New York."
Ibid., 170.

p. 91: "I will keep them hanging."
Ibid., 208.

p. 95: "Guard this object very carefully."
Gayford, Martin. *The Yellow House: Van Gogh, Gauguin, and Nine Turbulent Weeks in Provence*. Boston: Houghton Mifflin, 2008, 278.

p. 98: "quite personal"
Stringer, Sarah, Laurence Church, and Susan Davison. *Psychiatry PRN: Principles, Reality, Next Steps*. New York: Oxford University Press, 2009, 2.

p. 98: "I will keep quiet about this and so will you."
Kucharz, Christel. "The Real Story Behind Van Gogh's Severed Ear." May 5, 2009. http://abcnews.go.com/International/story?id=7506786. Accessed online on November 10, 2013.

p. 98: "A man with sealed lips, I cannot complain about him."
Kucharz, Christel. "The Real Story Behind van Gogh's Severed Ear." ABC News, May 5, 2009. http://abcnews.go.com/International/story?id=7506786. Accessed online December 12, 2014.

p. 99: "My body is mine and I am free to do what I want with it."
Letter from Adeline Ravoux to n/a Auvers-sur-Oise, 1956. http://www.webexhibits.org/vangogh/letter/21/etc-Adeline-Ravoux.htm. Accessed online on November 1, 2013.

p. 107: "nothing exceptional existing"
D'Agostino, Thomas. *A History of Vampires in New England*. Charleston, SC: History Press, 2010, 114.

p. 113: "one of the most charming specimens of female humanity"
Russell Warren Howe. *Mata Hari: The True Story*. New York: Dodd, Mead, 1986, 108.

p. 114: "all women who ran away from their husbands went to Paris"
Shipman, Pat. *Femme Fatale: Love, Lies, and the Unknown Life of Mata Hari.* New York: HarperCollins, 2014, 143.

p. 123: "negligence"
Paterniti, Michael. *Driving Mr. Albert: A Trip Across America with Einstein's Brain.* New York: Bantam Dell, 2005, 6.

p. 123: "It would be a sad situation if the wrapper were better than the meat wrapped inside it."
Yeatts, Tabatha. *Albert Einstein: The Miracle Mind.* New York: Sterling Biographies, 2007, 109.

p. 123: "I want to be cremated so people don't come to worship at my bones."
Ibid., 8.

p. 124: "a real trippy dude"
Ibid., viii.

p. 124: "laboratory"
Levy, Steven. "The Search for Einstein's Brain," *New Jersey Monthly*, August 1, 1978.

p. 125: "much too fat"
Ibid., 3.

p. 126: "thought experiments"
Bernstein, Jeremy. *Albert Einstein: And the Frontiers of Physics.* New York: Oxford University Press, 1996, 46.

p. 129: "It's not that I'm so smart, it's just that I stay with problems longer."
Einstein, Albert. BrainyQuote.com. http://www.brainyquote.com/quotes/quotes/a/alberteins
106192.html. Accessed online on 6/7/2014.

p. 130: "not above the ordinary for a man of Lincoln's size"
Sotos, John G. *The Physical Lincoln Complete: Comprising The Physical Lincoln 1.1a and The Physical Lincoln Sourcebook 1.1a.* Mt. Vernon, VA: Mt. Vernon Book Systems, 2008, 284.

p. 131: "dried and hardened in the skull"
Harris, Paul. "Fresh Clues Could Solve Mystery of Poe's Death." *The Observer*, October, 20, 2007.

p. 131: "nothing special"
Kaplan, Bernard. "Lenin's Genius Brain Turns Out to Be Just a Myth." *The Times-News* (Hendersonville, NC), January 22, 1994.

p. 134: "a wart with maybe sideburns"
Joni Mabe's Panoramic Museum of Everything Elvis. https://www.youtube.com/watch?v=
X17XgU7AscY. Accessed online on December 11, 2013.

p. 134: "I think it would be cruel to bring him back because he wouldn't have a mama. And he was really a mama's boy."
Ibid.

p. 135: "appreciate his kind of singing"
Hampton, Wilborn. *Elvis Presley.* New York: Puffin Books, 2008.

p. 137: "If he was, he would come see me."
Joni Mabe's Panoramic Museum of Everything Elvis.

p. 145: "A man must be either very drunk or very thirsty, before he would taste wine out of such a goblet."
Hawthorne, Nathaniel. *The Works of Nathaniel Hawthorne,* vol. 7. Boston: Houghton Mifflin, 1878–1899, 221.

p. 151: "Remember, sister, we all have to die."
Koudounaris, Paul. *The Empire of Death: A Cultural History of Ossuaries and Charnel Houses.* London, UK: Thames & Hudson, 2011, 86.

p. 161: "Addled"
Pederson, Charles E. *Thomas Edison.* Edina, MN: ABDO, 2008, 13.

p. 162: "Genius is one percent inspiration and ninety-nine percent perspiration."
ThinkExist.com. http://thinkexist.com/quotation/genius_is-inspiration_and-perspiration /146542.html. Accessed online on March 3, 2014.

p. 165: "an apparatus to see if it is possible for personalities which have left this earth to communicate with us."
Stephen, Wagner. "Edison and the Ghost Machine: The Great Inventor's Quest to Communicate with the dead." About Entertainment. http://paranormal.about.com/od/ghostaudiovideo/a /edison-ghost-machine.htm. Accessed online on March 5, 2014.

p. 165: "It's very beautiful over there."
Pederson, Charles E. *Thomas Edison,* 86.

SELECTED BIBLIOGRAPHY

Dead Bodies 101
(*The books that will give you strange looks from your librarian.*)
Benjamin, Kathy. *Funerals to Die For: The Craziest, Creepiest, and Most Bizarre Funeral Traditions and Practices Ever.* Avon, MA: Adams Media, 2013.
Bondeson, Jan. *Buried Alive: The Terrifying History of Our Most Primal Fear.* New York: W. W. Norton, 2002.
College of Physicians of Philadelphia, Lindgren, Laura, and Gretchen Worden. *Mütter Museum Historic Medical Photographs.* New York: Blast Books, 2007.
Colman, Penny. *Corpses, Coffins, and Crypts: A History of Burial.* New York: Henry Holt, 1997.
Fabian, Ann. *The Skull Collectors: Race, Science, and America's Unburied Dead.* Chicago: University of Chicago Press, 2010.
Harrington, Joel F. *The Faithful Executioner: Life and Death, Honor and Shame in the Turbulent Sixteenth Century.* New York: Picador, 2013.
Harris, Mark. *Grave Matters: A Journey Through the Modern Funeral Industry to a Natural Way of Burial.* New York: Scribner, 2007.
Iserson, V. Kenneth. *Death to Dust: What Happens to Dead Bodies?* Tucson, AZ: Galen Press, 2001.
Lovejoy, Bess. *Rest in Pieces: The Curious Fates of Famous Corpses.* New York: Simon & Schuster, 2013.
Maples, Williams R. *Dead Men Do Tell Tales.* New York: Doubleday, 1994.
Murphy, Edwin. *After the Funeral: The Posthumous Adventures of Famous Corpses.* New York: Carol, 1998.
Quigley, Christine. *The Corpse: A History.* Jefferson, NC: McFarland, 2005.
———. *Skulls and Skeletons: Human Bone Collections and Accumulations.* Jefferson, NC: McFarland, 2008.
Rachlin, Harvey. *Lucy's Bones, Sacred Stones, and Einstein's Brain: The Remarkable Stories Behind the Great Objects and Artifacts of History, From Antiquity to the Modern Era.* New Orleans: Garrett County Press, 2013.
Roach, Mary. *Stiff: The Curious Lives of Human Cadavers.* New York: W. W. Norton, 2004.
Schechter, Harold. *The Whole Death Catalog: A Lively Guide to the Bitter End.* New York: Ballantine Books, 2009.
Sugg, Richard. *Mummies, Cannibals, and Vampires: The History of Corpse Medicine from the Renaissance to the Victorians.* New York: Routledge, 2011.

Inês de Castro
Livermore, H. V. *A History of Portugal.* Cambridge, MA: Cambridge University Press. 1947.
Pillement, Georges. *Unknown Portugal.* London: Johnson, 1967.
Stephens, Henry Morse. *The Story of Portugal.* New York: G. P. Putnam's, 1891.

Loved to Death
Ahnlund, Nils. *Gustav Adolf the Great.* Translated by Michael Roberts. Princeton, NJ: Princeton University Press, 1940.
Aram, Bethany. *Juana the Mad: Sovereignty and Dynasty in Renaissance Europe.* Baltimore: Johns Hopkins University Press, 2005.
Buckley, Veronica. *Christina Queen of Sweden: The Restless Life of a European Eccentric.* London: Harper Perennial, 2004.
DuTemple, A. Lesley. *The Taj Mahal.* Minneapolis: Lerner, 2003.
Shelley, Percy Bysshe. *The Complete Poetical Works of P. B. Shelley.* London: C. Daly, 1839.

Galileo Galilei

Donadio, Rachel. "A Musuem Display of Galileo Has a Saintly Feel." *New York Times*, July 22, 2010.

"Galileo's Tooth, Thumb and Finger Go on Display." *Telegraph* (UK), June 8, 2010. http://www.telegraph.co.uk/news/worldnews/europe/italy/7812377/Galileos-tooth-thumb-and-finger-go-on-display.html. Accessed online October 8, 2015.

Sobel, Dava. *Galileo's Daughter: A Historical Memoir of Science, Faith and Love.* New York: Walker, 1999.

————. *A More Perfect Heaven: How Copernicus Revolutionized the Cosmos.* New York: Walker, 2011.

Invasion of the Body Snatchers

Bailey, James Blake. *The Diary of a Resurrectionist.* London: Library of Alexandria, 2014. Kindle edition.

Rosner, Lisa. *The Anatomy Murders: Being the True and Spectacular History of Edinburgh's Notorious Burke and Hare and of the Man of Science Who Abetted Them in the Commission of Their Most Heinous Crimes.* Philadelphia: University of Pennsylvania Press, 2009.

King Louis XIV

Jacob, Matthew, and Mark Jacob. *What the Great Ate: A Curious History of Food and Fame.* New York: Broadway Books, 2010.

Orléans, Charlotte-Elisabeth. *Memoirs of the Court of Louis XIV and of the Regency: Being the Secret Memoirs of Elizabeth-Charlotte, Duchesse d'Orléans, Mother of the Regent.* Boston: L. C. Page, 1899.

Racevskis, Roland. *Time and Ways of Knowing Under Louis XIV: Molière, Sévigné, Lafayette.* London: Associated University Presses, 2003.

Bon Appétit! Bites and Bits

Bryson, Bill. *At Home: A Short History of Private Life.* Toronto: Doubleday Canada, 2010.

Freedman, David H. "20 Things You Didn't Know About Autopsies." *Discovery*, September 2012, 72.

Morán, Elizabeth. "The Sacred as Everyday: Food and Ritual in Aztec Art." PhD diss., City University of New York, 2007.

Petrinovich, F. Lewis. *The Cannibal Within.* New York: Aldine de Gruyter, 2000.

Ruiz, Ana. *The Spirit of Ancient Egypt.* New York: Algora, 2001.

George Washington

Betts, William W., Jr. *The Nine Lives of George Washington.* Bloomington, IN: iUniverse, 2013, 145.

Chernow, Ron. *Washington: A Life.* New York: Penguin, 2010.

Ellis, Joseph J. *His Excellency: George Washington.* New York: Random House, 2004.

Ferling, John. *The Ascent of George Washington: The Hidden Political Genius of an American Icon.* New York: Bloomsbury, 2010.

George Washington's Mount Vernon. http://www.mountvernon.org. Accessed online on March 26, 2013.

The Papers of George Washington. http://gwpapers.virginia.edu. Accessed online on March 3, 2013.

Weinberger, Bernhard Wolf. *An Introduction to the History of Dentistry in America.* St. Louis: C. V. Mosby, 1948.

Writings of Washington. Archive.org, https://archive.org/stream/writingsofgeorge26wash/writingsofgeorge26wash_djvu.txt. Accessed online on June 5, 2013.

Buried . . . but Not Quite Dead

Bondeson, Jan. *Buried Alive: The Terrifying History of Our Most Primal Fear.* New York: W. W. Norton, 2002.

McCarthy, Tony. *The Facts of Death.* Cork, Ireland: Belgrave, 2006.

Franz Joseph Haydn

Dickey, Colin. *Cranioklepty: Grave Robbing and the Search for Genius.* Lakewood, CO: Unbridled Books, 2010.

Geiringer, Karl, with Irene Geiringer. *Haydn: A Creative Life in Music.* Berkeley: University of California Press, 1982.

"Haydn's Skull Is Returned." *LIFE* magazine, June 28, 1954.

Phrenology

Finger, Stanley. *Minds Behind the Brain: A History of the Pioneers and Their Discoveries.* New York: Oxford University Press, 2004.

Graham, Patrick. (2001) *Phrenology* [videorecording (DVD)]: revealing the mysteries of the mind. Richmond Hill, ON: American Home Treasures.

Ludwig van Beethoven

Lockwood, Lewis. *Beethoven: The Music and the Life.* New York: W. W. Norton, 2005, 2003.

Martin, Russell. *Beethoven's Hair: An Extraordinary Historical Odyssey and a Scientific Mystery Solved.* New York: Broadway Books, 2000.

Morris, Edmund. *Beethoven: The Universal Composer.* New York: Harper Collins, 2005.

Weiss, Philip. "Beethoven's Hair Tells All!" *New York Times*, November 29, 1998.

Some Hairy History

"Channel 4 documentary *Dead Famous DNA* reveals Charles Darwin suffered from Crohn's disease." *Mirror.* http://www.mirror.co.uk/tv/tv-news/dead-famous-dna-charles-darwin -3337775#ixzz3Fao0QLQm. Accessed online August 10, 2014.

"Channel 4 show 'discovers cause of Elvis Presley's death.'" *Guardian* (London). March 25, 2014.

Results of Tests on the Hair of Virginia and Edgar A. Poe. http://www.eapoe.org/geninfo /poethair.htm Accessed online on August 5, 2014.

Abraham Lincoln

Craughwell, Thomas J. *Stealing Lincoln's Body.* Cambridge, MA: Harvard University Press, 2007.

Guelzo, Allen C. *Fateful Lightning: A New History of the Civil War and Reconstruction.* New York: Oxford University Press, 2012.

Power, J. C. *History of an Attempt to Steal the Body of Abraham Lincoln.* Springfield, IL: H. W. Rokker, 1890.

Pickling Picks

Boyd, Carl R., MD. *The Assassination of Abraham Lincoln: The True Story Your Teacher Did Not Tell You.* Bloomington, IN: Trafford, 2011.

Harris, Tom. "How Mummies Work." http://science.howstuffworks.com/mummy4.htm. Accessed online on July 28, 2013.

Lovejoy, Bess. *Rest in Pieces: The Curious Fates of Famous Corpses.* New York: Simon & Schuster, 2013.

Quigley, Christine. *The Corpse: A History.* Jefferson, NC: McFarland, 2005.

Taylor, John H. *Death and the Afterlife in Ancient Egypt.* Chicago: University of Chicago Press, 2001.

Chang and Eng Bunker

Hartzman, Marc. *American Sideshow: An Encyclopedia of History's Most Wondrous and Curiously Strange Performers.* New York: Penguin, 2006.

Irving, Wallace, and Amy Wallace. *The Two: A Biography of the Original Siamese Twins.* New York: Simon & Schuster, 1978.

Orser, Joseph Andrew. *The Lives of Chang and Eng: Siam's Twins in Nineteenth-Century America.* Chapel Hill: University of North Carolina Press, 2014.

It's Fun to Share

Lock, Margaret M. *Twice Dead: Organ Transplants and the Reinvention of Death.* Berkeley: University of California Press, 2001.

Roach, Mary. *Stiff: The Curious Lives of Human Cadavers.* New York: W. W. Norton, 2004.

Phineas Gage

Fleischman, John. *Phineas Gage: A Gruesome but True Story About Brain Science.* Boston: Houghton Mifflin, 2002.

Macmillan, Malcolm. *An Odd Kind of Fame: Stories of Phineas Gage.* Cambridge, MA: MIT Press, 2000.

Pliss, Todd Colby. *The Only Living Man with a Hole in His Head.* Niles, OH: SB Addison, 2011.

Stabbed in the Brain: Phineas Gage. https://www.youtube.com/watch?v=FrULrWRlGBA. Accessed online on May 6, 2014.

Bury the Hatchet and Then Some

The Search for Immortality: Tomb Treasures of Han China. The Fitzwilliam Museum. http://www.tombtreasuresofhanchina.org/the-exhibition/han-empire/the-han-dynasty Accessed online on August 8, 2014.

Skal, J. David. *Bela Lugosi, Hollywood's Dark Prince.* Biography Channel. Oct. 1995.

Taylor, John H. *Death and the Afterlife in Ancient Egypt.* Chicago: University of Chicago Press, 2001.

Waldman, Suzanne Maureen. *The Demon & the Damozel : Dynamics of Desire in the Works of Christina Rossetti and Dante Gabriel Rossetti.* Athens: Ohio University Press, 2008.

John Wilkes Booth

Goodrich, Thomas. *The Darkest Dawn: Lincoln, Booth, and the Great American Tragedy.* Bloomington: Indiana University Press, 2005.

Kauffman, Michael W. *American Brutus: John Wilkes Booth and the Lincoln Conspiracies.* New York: Random House, 2005.

Nottingham, Theodore J. *The Curse of Cain: The Untold Story of John Wilkes Booth.* Newbury, West Berkshire, UK: Sovereign, 1998.

Swanson, James L. *Manhunt: The 12-Day Chase to Catch Lincoln's Killer.* New York: HarperCollins, 2009.

Another Spiny Tale

Ashdown-Hill, John. *The Last Days of Richard III and the Fate of His DNA.* Stroud, England: History Press, 2013.

Langley, Philippa, and Michael Jones. *The King's Grave: The Search for Richard III.* London: John Murray, 2013.

Sarah Bernhardt

De Costa, Caroline. *The Diva and Doctor God: Letters from Sarah Bernhardt to Doctor Samuel Pozzi.* Xlibris, 2010.

Gold, Arthur, and Robert Fizdale. *The Divine Sarah: A Life of Sarah Bernhardt.* New York: Knopf, 1991.

Gottlieb, Robert. *Sarah: The Life of Sarah Bernhardt.* New Haven: Yale University Press, 2010.

Pollard, Justin. *Charge!: The Interesting Bits of Military History.* London: Hodder & Stoughton, 2008.

Silverthorne, Elizabeth. *Sarah Bernhardt.* Philadelphia: Chelsea House, 2004.

You're Pulling My Leg

Lost and Found. History Channel. Episode 1, Airdate 8/7/1999.

Notes & Queries. 3rd S. II, September 27, 1862, p 249.

Vincent van Gogh

Druick, Douglas W. *Van Gogh and Gauguin: The Studio of the South.* London: Thames & Hudson, 2001.

Gayford, Martin. *The Yellow House: Van Gogh, Gauguin, and Nine Turbulent Weeks in Provence.* Boston: Houghton Mifflin, 2008.

Naifeh, Steven, and Gregory White Smith. *Van Gogh: The Life.* New York: Random House, 2011.

Suh, H. Anna. *Vincent Van Gogh: A Self-Portrait in Art and Letters.* New York: Black Dog & Leventhal, 2006.

Artsy Extras

Boyle, Alan. "'Mona Lisa' Skeleton and Her Kin's Remains Are Due for DNA Testing." NBC News. Aug 9, 2013. http://www.nbcnews.com/science/science-news/mona-lisa-skeleton-her-kins -remains-are-due-dna-testing-f6C10874613. Accessed online on August 12, 2014.

Burns, Stanley B. *Sleeping Beauty: Memorial Photography in America.* Altadena, CA: Twelvetrees, 1990.

Grange, Jeremy. "Resusci Anne and L'Inconnue: The Mona Lisa of the Seine." BBC News. October 15, 2013. http://www.bbc.com/news/magazine-24534069. Accessed online on October 15, 2013.

Murphy, Edwin. *After the Funeral: The Posthumous Adventures of Famous Corpses.* New York: Citadel, 1995.

Quigley, Christine. *Skulls and Skeletons: Human Bone Collections and Accumulations.* Jefferson, NC: McFarland, 2001.

Richardson, Matt. *The Royal Book of Lists: An Irreverent Romp Through British Royal History from Alfred the Great to Prince William.* Toronto, ON: Hounslow, 2001.

Mercy Brown

Bell, E. Michael. *Food for the Dead: On the Trail of New England's Vampires.* Middletown, CT: Wesleyan University Press, 2011.

D'Agostino, Thomas. *A History of Vampires in New England.* Charleston, SC: History Press, 2010.

Hellman, Roxanne, and Derek Hall. *Vampire Legends and Myths.* New York: Rosen, 2012.

Tucker, Abigail. "The Great New England Vampire Panic." *Smithsonian,* October 2012. http://www.smithsonianmag.com/history/the-great-new-england-vampire-panic-36482878 /?no-ist. Accessed online on May 8, 2014.

The Dead vs. the Undead

Bell, E. Michael. *Food for the Dead: On the Trail of New England's Vampires.* Middletown, CT: Wesleyan University Press, 2011.

Mata Hari

Howe, Russell Warren. *Mata Hari: The True Story.* New York: Dodd, Mead, 1986.

Samuels, Diane. *The True Life Fiction of Mata Hari.* London: Nick Hern, 2002.

Shipman, Pat. *Femme Fatale: Love, Lies, and the Unknown Life of Mata Hari.* New York: HarperCollins, 2014.

Lost and Never Found

Bibeau, Paul. *Sundays with Vlad: From Pennsylvania to Transylvania, One Man's Quest to Live in the World of the Undead.* New York: Broadway Books, 2007.

Chugg, Andrew. *The Quest for the Tomb of Alexander the Great.* Boston: AMC, 2012.

Kluger, Jeffrey, and Andrea Dorfman. "Nefertiti Found?" *Time.* http://content.time.com/time /magazinearticle/0,9171,457370,00.html. Accessed online on June 23, 2014.

Langley, Philippa, and Michael Jones. *The King's Grave: The Discovery of Richard III's Lost Burial Place and the Clues It Holds.* New York: St. Martin's, 2013.

Levy, Joel. *Lost Histories: In Search of Vanished Places, Treasures, and People*. New York: Barnes & Noble, 2007.

Albert Einstein
Isaacson, Walter. *Einstein: His Life and Universe*. London: Simon & Schuster UK, 2007.
Paterniti, Michael. *Driving Mr. Albert: A Trip Across America with Einstein's Brain*. New York: Bantam Dell, 2005.
Yeatts, Tabatha. *Albert Einstein: The Miracle Mind*. New York: Sterling Biographies, 2007.

Bits on Brains
Harris, Paul. "Fresh Clues Could Solve Mystery of Poe's Death." *The Observer*. October, 20, 2007.
Kaplan, Bernard. "Lenin's Genius Brain Turns Out to Be Just a Myth." *The Times-News* (Hendersonville, NC), January 22, 1994.
Sotos, John G. *The Physical Lincoln Complete: Comprising The Physical Lincoln 1.1a and The Physical Lincoln Sourcebook 1.1a*. Mt. Vernon, VA: Mt. Vernon Book Systems, 2008.

Elvis Presley
Guralnick, Peter. *Careless Love: The Unmaking of Elvis Presley*. Boston: Back Bay Books, 2000.
Hampton, Wilborn. *Elvis Presley*. New York: Puffin Books, 2008.
Keogh, Pamela Clarke. *Elvis Presley: The Man. The Life. The Legend.* New York: Simon & Schuster, 2004.
Watson, James D., and Andrew Berry. *DNA: The Secret of Life*. New York: Knopf, 2009.

Cloning Body Parts
Elenbaas, Cornelis J. F. *LN2: Cryogenic Freezing Manual*. Victoria, BC: Trafford, 2008.

Recycling Bits
Arlandson, Lee. "When 'Big Nose' George Parrott Was Hung." *Pioneer West*, June 1972.
Harrington, Joel F. *The Faithful Executioner: Life and Death, Honor and Shame in the Turbulent Sixteenth Century*. New York: Picador, 2013.
Hawthorne, Nathaniel. *The Works of Nathaniel Hawthorne*, vol. 7. Boston: Houghton Mifflin, 1878–1899.
Wynbrandt, James. *The Excruciating History of Dentistry: Toothsome Tales & Oral Oddities from Babylon to Braces*. New York: St. Martin's, 1998.

A Happily Ever Afterlife
Bradlee, Ben. *The Kid: The Immortal Life of Ted Williams*. New York: Little, Brown, 2013.
Casarett, David Jr. *Shocked: Adventures in Bringing Back the Recently Dead*. New York: Current, 2014.
Roach, Mary. *Stiff: The Curious Lives of Human Cadavers*. New York: W. W. Norton, 2003.

The Most Wanted
Axelrod, Alan. *Little-Known Wars of Great and Lasting Impact*. Beverly, MA: Fair Winds, 2009.
DeArment, Robert K. *Assault on the Deadwood Stage: Road Agents and Shotgun Messengers*. Norman: University of Oklahoma Press, 2011.
DeLeon, Clark. *Pennsylvania Curiosities: Quirky Characters, Roadside Oddities & Other Offbeat Stuff*. Guilford, CT: Globe Pequot, 2013.
Elze, Karl Friedrich. *Lord Byron, A Biography, with a Critical Essay on His Place in Literature*. Charleston, SC: Forgotten Books, 2012.
Foster, R. E. *Wellington and Waterloo: The Duke, The Battle and Posterity, 1815–2015*. New York: History Press, 2014.

Harrington, Joel F. *The Faithful Executioner: Life and Death, Honor and Shame in the Turbulent Sixteenth Century*. New York: Farrar, Straus and Giroux, 2013.

Corpse Medicine

León, Vicki. *How to Mellify a Corpse: And Other Human Stories of Ancient Science & Superstition*. New York: Walker, 2010.

Quigley, Christine. *The Corpse: A History*. Jefferson, NC: McFarland, 1996.

Sugg, Richard. *Mummies, Cannibals, and Vampires: The History of Corpse Medicine from the Renaissance to the Victorians*. New York: Routledge, 2011.

Deathly Decor

Koudounaris, Paul. *The Empire of Death: A Cultural History of Ossuaries and Charnel Houses*. New York: Thames & Hudson, 2011.

Quigley, Christine. *The Corpse: A History*. Jefferson, NC: McFarland, 1996.

Dead-End Jobs

Benjamin, Kathy. *Funerals to Die For: The Craziest, Creepiest, and Most Bizarre Funeral Traditions and Practices Ever*. Avon, MA: Adams Media, 2013.

Harrington, Joel F. *The Faithful Executioner: Life and Death, Honor and Shame in the Turbulent Sixteenth Century*. New York: Picador, 2013.

Iserson, V. Kenneth. *Death to Dust: What Happens to Dead Bodies*. Tucson, AZ: Galen, 2001.

León, Vicki. *Working IX to V: Orgy Planners, Funeral Clowns, and Other Prized Professions of the Ancient World*. New York: Bloomsbury, 2013.

Robinson, Tony, and David Willcock. *The Worst Jobs in History: Two Thousand Years of Miserable Employment*. London: Boxtree, 2004.

Unloved Bits

DeLeon, Clark. *Pennsylvania Curiosities: Quirky Characters, Roadside Oddities & Other Offbeat Stuff*. Guilford, CT: Globe Pequot, 2013.

Roach, Mary. *Gulp: Adventures on the Alimentary Canal*. London: Oneworld, 2013.

Thomas Alva Edison

Bryan, Ford R. *Henry's Attic: Some Fascinating Gifts to Henry Ford and His Museum*. Detroit: Wayne State University Press, 2006.

Newton, James. *Uncommon Friends: Life with Thomas Edison, Henry Ford, Harvey Firestone, Alexis Carrel, and Charles Lindbergh*. San Diego, CA: Harcourt Brace Jovanovich, 1987.

Pederson, Charles E. *Thomas Edison*. Edina, MN: ABDO, 2008.

Stross, Randall E. *The Wizard of Menlo Park: How Thomas Alva Edison Invented the Modern World*. New York: Three Rivers, 2007.

Go on, get out!
Last words are for fools who haven't said enough.
—**Karl Marx**

INDEX

182